Yall Betta
CONSIDER
God
...Im Jus Sayn

Briggette Johnson & Denies Goodman

ISBN 978-1-957956-18-3 (Paperback)
ISBN 978-1-957956-19-0 (Ebook)

Inquiries and Book Orders should be addressed to:

Leavitt Peak Press
17901 Pioneer Blvd Ste L #298,
Artesia, California 90701
Phone #: 2092191548

Take A Moment…Consider God

Take a moment to motivate your mind
as you are led down the path that finds
God who is simply amazing in the way He chooses
to divulge the purpose in the vessel He uses
Trust in the Lord with all thine heart.
And lean not unto thine own understanding.
In all thy ways acknowledge him,
and he shall direct thy paths.
(Proverbs 3:5-6) KJV

The Dream…

In the distance, the chirping of birds could be heard. As the warm rays of the sun cascaded down through the morning dew, supplied was the daily nourishment to the surface of the earth. Also favored, with a gentle caress on the face were two sisters. Their feet had been planted in a picturesque meadow. Seen were the tall yellow heads of Goldenrods, as well as other wildflowers mixed with native grasses and shrubs. The sheer beauty of it all inspired them to partake of it with enthusiastic gallops and a purity of heart filled with grins and giggles. But what pierced through that captivating canvas more than anything else was that they held hands the whole time, purposeful in their intent to not leave the other behind.

Introduction

Lola gazed into her mother's eyes in complete silence, only terror and fear filled both of their eyes. A decision had to be made. Her mother wanted to run and get help, but she too was familiar with the poundings Silas (the boogie man to Lola) would inflict on her. Reaching for the door handle, Lola's mother turned, and looked at her. Lola looked into her mother's eyes with true terror, knowing her decision was to run. In Lola's mind, if The Boogie Man saw her mother trying to escape, he would chase her down and kill her. Lola's petrified voice begged, "please don't leave me". Her mother looked into her tear-filled eyes and released the handle.

Contents

Scenario 1

The Skill to Survive

"Imagine picking up and leaving everything you've ever known for love. Not only did Ingrid leave her native land, but she also entered a realm full of racism, social injustice, and prejudice, all to be with the man she loved, a black man."

Ingrid was born in the Winter of 1938 in Europe. Raised by her grandparents, she often missed her mother and siblings who got separated amid the social unrest. Her father was a stranger to her.

As a teenager Ingrid became the type of person who would try anything and stayed in trouble with her grandparents because of it. Her grandfather had a fetish for young girls, and it often made Ingrid wonder what length he was willing to go to because of it.

Ingrid's grandmother provided weekend shelter for the minority GI's who got weekend leave. This gave Ingrid access to explore her own curiosities. Ingrid eventually set her eyes on a young and handsome gent named Jasper who became an admirer of hers as well.

Jasper was a country boy from the dirty south. He grew up a middle child of many. He lost his mother to an illness before he was grown.

His dad being the sole breadwinner kept him away from home for most of the day which left he and his siblings to be raised by his sister, the eldest of them all. Jasper was easily frightened by things of a scary nature because of the tricks his siblings would play on him. When the time came to decide what step to take as an adult, Jasper decided to enter the military.

Jasper was excited to see what the world outside his norm had to offer. He was stationed in Europe. During his tour of duty is when he set his sights on Ingrid. They met and soon became inseparable when he had free time. They would meet up at the local social gathering spot and Jasper would use the charismatic approach he learned on Ingrid. When they danced, he would serenade Ingrid with a voice as velvet as Nat Cole. It did not take long for Ingrid to get attached and stay that way. The two eventually married so when Jasper's tour ended, he and Ingrid made their way back to the states.

Upon returning, Jasper was stationed on the opposite coast of his family so that gave Ingrid time to learn the American way of doing things. After a couple of years of honeymoon life, Jasper and Ingrid were pregnant with their first child. Before the baby's arrival, Jasper was sent away to serve his country once again. Ingrid had formed friendships on base where they lived so once she went into labor, her friends made sure she made it to the hospital safe and sound. While the baby was being born, Jasper was given permission to return to base to see his newborn child. He was so excited. When he arrived at the hospital, he eagerly ran to the window to view who he was hoping would be his first-born son but was instead let down to find an adorable and healthy baby girl named Lola.

Not long after Lola was born, Jasper was stationed on the east coast down south. It was the mid 60's so you would think Jasper had some serious explaining to do to his family. They had their reservations nonetheless Ingrid was welcomed with open arms. Ingrid had a way of captivating her audience using her hearty sense of humor and wit. She soon became the sister-in-law his family adored.

Living in the south took its toll on Ingrid and Jasper's relationship. Amid racial tension and prejudice, Ingrid was subjected to some dehumanizing experiences. While traveling together by car, there were times when Ingrid would have to ride in the trunk of the car while passing through certain towns. Then there were the times while out with her daughter she would be called a nigger lover. Ingrid grew a thick skin and adapted appropriately but there was one time that she refused to tuck her tail and leave.

A female bystander began spewing insults at Ingrid regarding her half breed daughter but instead of avoiding the bystander, she confronted her and dared her to say it again. Before the bystander could finish her first word, Ingrid started swinging. That moment planted the seed in Ingrid what would later blossom into not taking mess anymore, not even from Jasper whose attitude evolved into using physical abuse towards Ingrid and Lola to settle his frustration for not living up to being the man he introduced Ingrid to.

Ingrid eventually divorced Jasper and began to live the life she was not able to while married. There was a lot to be learned from her experiences but instead of grabbing hold of what not to do going forward, Ingrid grabbed hold of the dysfunction dangled before her and she ran with that instead.

Many of Ingrid's endeavors enticed her to take the shortcuts she learned by becoming a master manipulator. Ingrid always kept a job yet would maintain some sort of hustle to keep her and her daughter comfortably afloat.

Her weakness however were always men. This is where not having a strong male foundation in her life came back to haunt her. For Ingrid, the necessity for acceptance from a male, was more important than she thought. The lack of self-respect fell under her radar meanwhile the mask of pleasure was worn for all to see. Even though it was happening to her, she found herself being the manipulator with men. The three identifiable steps she implemented was detecting their weakness, using that weakness against them, then convincing them to give her that which was self-serving to her. She became blinded in both eyes, one eye for him manipulating her and the other eye, her manipulating him. Thinking back, it was not much different from prostitution, she pimped herself out. She had no time to see or think clearly because she was too busy keeping up.

Scenario 2

The Epic Fail

"Imagine being born into the world with a father that wanted a son for his first child and no matter how cute you were, the so- called tough love was just a little too damn tough. As a child, Lola realized early on that she would have to be a fighter to survive. Watching her mother beaten by her father and then boy-friend was too much for a 6-year-old girl to handle."

Lola was born in the summer of the early 60's to Jasper and Ingrid. People say that names have meaning. Lola means sorrows. Lola never thought her name would represent her life experiences. She would experience many sorrows in her young life that would make her live up to that name. The first experience was hearing later in life that when Jasper arrived at the hospital, he came straight to the maternity ward, looked in the window, saw that the baby was a girl, waved his hand in discontent and went overseas. Lola basically did not see him again until she was two years old. This marked the beginning of her abandonment issues.

Why would you leave me...why would you deceive me?
What did I do to you?
that made you leave until I was two.
I never asked to be here.
But I expected you to care
So, I was not what you wanted...a boy
Well, my heart is not a toy
I am your daughter, the first you ever had
So, the very least you could have been...was glad.

Once Jasper was discharged from service, they moved up north where Lola's dreadful memories continued like waking up to the sounds of her parent's constant arguing then hearing commotion and weeping.

Lola was too young to realize what was happening, so she would return to sleep and later awaken to the summons of breakfast being ready. Watching her mother fix the plates with the slight limp and a defeated look in her eyes was an experience that ended up seeming normal as did many other days.

The older Lola got, the sicker and more tired she became of the abuse. Jasper kept the physical assaults in the dark for a while, but as time went on, he brought it out into the open. Not only with Ingrid, but eventually with Lola also.

Mommy what are you doing
Why are you allowing this man to ruin us?
See...it's not just you affected right now.
I am feeling neglected and unprotected
We gotta get out of here
Let's go somewhere, anywhere
I hate this fear

When Jasper had a bad day, Lola began noticing he would come home mad. One time, he yelled at her to open the window. Petrified, she tried with all her might, but the window would not open. Too afraid to say she couldn't, she hoped and prayed he had forgotten about it. She stayed quiet as cotton, trying to lift that window.

Minutes went by which to Lola seemed like an eternity. She then tried to lift the window again but failed. Before she knew it, she felt a burning sensation across her back, arms, and legs. She began screaming and jogging in place as the belt struck her tiny hands trying to block the intensity of the strap landing on her skin. She exhaled again once it was over. With numb legs, numb arms, a numb back, and a numb bottom, over time she became thankful for the numbness unaware that her heart was also becoming numb. Many days like those were on the horizon for Lola and Ingrid.

Lola matured much faster than other girls her age. From all the abuse received, not only did her body harden, but so did her emotions.

> *To witness your mother being abused*
> *Can leave you traumatized and confused*
> *Because this is the man who said he loved us*
> *but to get out of the house, would fuss and cuss*
> *If that did not work would throw a jab*
> *Then, as if nothing happened would hop in a cab*
> *to see his side piece and get his release*
> *Without a care of how this affected his daughter*
> *He had no clue what his actions just taught her.*

Because Lola's experience affected her behavior, getting a beating was eventually given to her daily. He would command her to get up and get ready for school and she would jump up without hesitation. Because her behavior was not improving at school, Jasper decided he would nip it in the bud and chastise her before school. That soon became the routine so she would mentally prepare for what was coming. Like perfect timing, the belt, and his words both felt and sounded like he was enjoying it a little too much. Jasper's reasoning was that since she wanted to act up in school, he would beat her every day until she acted right, but her mind was on a different level. The

7

way Lola figured it; she could do whatever she wanted because she had already gotten her beating for the day.

One day, Jasper did not care for what Ingrid cooked for dinner, so he beat her. The only thing Lola could think to do was try to defend and protect her mother. Lola grabbed a belt and started hitting Jasper, but it did not work. Then, in a desperate panic she grabbed the closest thing to her, a butter knife on the table. She figured if she could get his attention, he would stop assaulting her mother, but that did not work either. The only option left was for her to scream so she yelled, "WHY DON'T YOU HIT HIM BACK MA". That is when Ingrid grabbed a chair as she was being tossed and hit him in the head. Down he went. Lola was simply happy it was over.

The Boogie Man

"Talk about stepping out of the frying pan, into the fire! Lola was happy that her mother FINALLY left her father and what did she go and do? Ingrid met a man that to Lola, looked like a monster. If that was not bad enough, he acted like one too. His name was Silas. Clearly Ingrid's picker was broken."

Lola experienced hatred at an early age. In 1st grade, her classmates had no problem showing their dislike for her. Lola chalked it up to jealousy because of how she looked. She was considered a half breed because her ethnicity was a mixture of African American and Caucasian. Her skin tone was caramel brown, her hair was down to her waist, black as coal and wavy like waves in the ocean. So, the eye rolling, and whispering also became a part of her daily routine.

One day while in school, she ate a hot dog with peaches and milk for lunch. Going about the rest of her class time as normal, once the last bell rang, school let out and she proceeded to walk home. As she approached the halfway mark home, her head started spinning and she fainted. When she opened her eyes, her mother was picking her up to take her home. As she laid on the bed, the ceiling started spinning and she fainted again. Coming to for the second time, with groggy eyes and stuffy ears, the next words she heard were from the doctor. He advised Ingrid that Lola had been drugged. This further advanced the dysfunction surrounding her life.

My surroundings were just a disguise
Hiding generational curses full of lust and lies
Whatever it is I am yearning for comes from deep within
But each time I think I have found it,
Nope...here I go again

A couple of days passed, and Lola returned to school as normal. When the dismissal bell rang, the kids all ran out of the school like it was the last day. While walking down the street, Lola noticed Jasper leaning against a tree across the street. Instead of running to him, she ran home and told her mother what she saw. Silas overhearing it, reached above the door frame and grabbed a hatchet and stormed out the door.

Lola and Ingrid looked at each other with confusion and fear not knowing what was going to happen. Lola did not know for sure whether her mother was worried or not, but even though her father's love was tough, she admitted that she was worried. By the time Silas got to where Jasper had been standing, Jasper was long gone.

That following weekend, there was a block party in the neighborhood with music, food, and fun. That night, Silas instructed Lola not to leave the block because he had an errand to run. Lola said ok and went on enjoying the festivities. She was playing double- dutch jump rope when Silas returned. One of the girls in the neighborhood told him that Lola went around the corner. She pleaded with him that the girl was lying but he wouldn't believe her. He grabbed the rope, doubled it up and began beating Lola.

Once out of his grip, Lola ran as fast as she could towards the house. The rope kept hitting her back, legs, arms as he continued chasing her and swinging at the same time. As soon as she entered the house, Ingrid noticed what was happening and tried to stop him, but he slammed her head against the corner of the wooden arm rest of the couch. Once he saw her bleeding, he stopped and left the house. From that moment on, Lola had to go everywhere Silas went because he was afraid that Ingrid would flee while he was away.

One time when Silas, Ingrid and Lola arrived at a tall building about fifteen stories high, he and Ingrid went inside while Lola stayed in the car with a friend of his. What seemed liked hours had passed; Lola finally saw her mother coming out of the building with Silas. As she got closer to the car, Lola noticed that her mother was limping, and her makeup was smeared on her face as if she had been crying. Ingrid got in the back seat, and nothing was said. It was not until later in life that Lola realized that Silas had trafficked her mother for his own personal gain.

The boogie man was a myth meant for fun
but to me, he came in the form of someone
Who stole us, tried to kill my mother
and destroy our family clan.
But what he was unaware of is that
God had devised a plan
So why did God allow all that to take place
All I know is without trauma, how would we identify grace?

On a separate occasion, Lola was awakened by the sound of screaming and crying. She sprinted to the door to see what was going on, but it was locked from the outside. There was a big glass window that separated Lola's room from the room that Silas and Ingrid shared. Lola ran back to her bed. Terrified and silent, Lola saw the shadow of footsteps running past her door. Ingrid ran past and locked herself in the bathroom. Silas was pulling on the bathroom doorknob and thrusting his shoulders into the door attempting to bust it open. Lola shook the door to her room repeatedly attempting to loosen the top latch. When she shook the door again, it opened. Lola ran and snuck out the front door. It was dark and late at night, but she knew she had to do something. Silas' candy store was a block away.

When Lola arrived at the front door of the candy store, she tried to figure out how to get in to use the pay phone to call the operator for help. She looked down and around for anything she could use to get inside and found a rock. She took that rock and busted out the window, went inside and called the only phone number she knew... zero.

When the operator answered and could tell Lola was a child, she asked what was wrong. Lola told the operator that her mother was being beat up by her boyfriend. When the operator asked for his name, Lola referred to him as The Boogie Man, but when she thought about it, she gave the operator his real name and hung up. Lola ran back to the house, got back in bed, and waited.

Because Silas heard police sirens, he panicked and told Lola and Ingrid to get up and get in the car. As they were leaving, he passed his store and noticed the window was broken. He stopped and got out to investigate. Ingrid started to get out of the car and run. She looked into Lola's eyes and saw tears running down her cheeks. Ingrid looked down and released the handle.

So many mistakes made
So much dysfunctional foundation laid
With no attention paid to what is really going on... Why us?

The beatings from Silas went on for months, however the night came when all hell broke loose. Once again, Lola could hear the muffled sound of her mother crying. It sounded as if she was being choked. Because the latch on the outside of Lola's room door kept her contained, she peeked through the crack in the curtained window that separated their rooms. She looked in and there Silas was, choking

Ingrid and beating her with a belt. He finally passed out, probably from exhaustion. That moment allowed Ingrid to sneak out of the house and leave. Lola could not believe it; she thought her mother was abandoning her. She did not know what to think. She only prayed that Silas would not never, ever wake up.

After about an hour, which felt like days had passed. Ingrid returned. Lola was relieved, not only to see her mother but also the police escort. Strangers with guns in holsters, walkie talkies constantly chirping, entering in, and taking control of the situation. That night Lola realized what The Boogie Man was afraid of. When the police asked Ingrid if there was anything she wanted to take, she said… just my daughter. Because Jasper had already moved out of state, one of his brothers were notified, and he rescued them. Lola and Ingrid stayed at her uncle's house until they moved out of state and back with Jasper.

Once they reconnected with Jasper, it started out ok. The best part of their reconnection was that Lola's baby sister was born. Unfortunately, not long after, the beatings started up again. Ingrid finally got sick and tired of being sick and tired. Jasper would threaten to have Ingrid sent back to where she was from and threaten to take the kids, so Ingrid bid her time and secretly got her citizenship.

The experiences were horrible indeed
But the purpose for the pain outweighed the need
Because we are so interwoven with another
Our experience could very well save the lives of others

Scenario 3

Disappointed

**"What do you do with the bits and pieces of
sustained memories? Like a memory of laying
down, looking up at the ceiling (possibly tod-
dler age) and a memory of excruciating pain.
That is all Piper remembers about it, but it
would haunt her thoughts for years to come."**

By the time Piper was five, fear was that inevitable emotion that
crept in and paralyzed her constantly reminding her of the worst
that could possibly happen. Fear eventually became her master of
thoughts. Piper's father, on the other hand, was her hero. When Piper
cried, she cried for him. When she got hurt, she ran to him.

Once Piper got a little older, she was unsure as to why she considered
her dad her hero except for the fact that he was her dad. He was a
man who could capture your attention and keep you laughing for
hours. But behind closed doors, he had a past full of demons he
refused to face and because of that, what was in him came out of
him, and it was usually directed at Pipers mom. Yet after all he had
done to her, in Pipers eyes, he could do no wrong despite doing most
things wrong.

What he was supposed to instill, he didn't
Making me use to those who wouldn't
I got content with all the mess
Comfortable settling for less

Piper remembered broken promises by her father that occurred often after her parents divorced. The feeling of disappointment felt as agonizing as literally being struck because as a child, Piper believed whole heartedly what she was told. If you told her the sky was falling...she would duck.

The first love of my life...
The first man by whom I'd be led
Instead of living as an example...
Tore my heart to shreds

Life continued as usual for Piper. She and her sister spent many summers traveling with their aunt and uncle. The summer she would never forget ended after their return. The problem inside of her started when she never returned to what she knew to be home. Her mom picked them up with a "friend" of hers. When Piper asked where her dad was, her mother responded that they were not going back to that house, in an assertive tone.

As a child, all Piper could think about was how alone and sad her dad must have been in that house because they were not coming home. The disappointment that welled up in her eventually turned into anger towards her mom. Not the kind that lashed out though. No, it was the kind that subtly judged and festered over the years. Besides the fact that her mom had abandoned Jasper (in Piper's mind), she obviously had a new boyfriend. Where did he come from? Then like a ton of falling bricks, Piper was struck with the word Divorce.

It took time, but Piper eventually grew to understand that the distance she felt, even when in her mom's presence, was due to the resentment that remained constricted inside of her for the way Ingrid handled the situation. Piper never once in all those years considered the excruciating hell her mom must have gone through.

> *I have come to the realization*
> *That we are duped into living life for mere presentation*
> *Said are the right things most of the time*
> *Yet held hostage are we in our mind*

Waking up to new surroundings took Piper some getting used to. Being uprooted so suddenly was intimidating. Leaving behind the things and people that she had become comfortable with forced the normalcy of her dysfunction to be renovated.

Her mom moved them into an efficiency apartment next to an alternative lifestyle resort. This gave the neighboring dysfunctional kids' exposure to some very unsettling moments.

> *One thing life has taught me.*
> *Just because you look don't mean you see.*
> *Just because you exist don't mean you be.*
> *Just because there's no shackle*
> *don't mean you free.*

Piper remembered having to flee from where they lived in the middle of the night because Ingrid owed the complex money. By this time, that "boyfriend" was gone, and another was introduced into their lives. Friends of her mom also helped them move. On a positive note, the move was a major step up from that efficiency.

Piper was happy with it until the cops knocked on their door with an arrest warrant for her mom. As it turned out, when they fled, the landlord that lived on property approached her mom as to stop her from leaving and she pushed the landlord down, so the landlord pressed charges. Piper seeing her mom leave with those police was very frightening. Piper and her sister remained with a neighbor until her mom made it back home that same day.

Pipers' experiences at her new home, for the most part were pleasant ones. The problem that she had, without yet realizing it was that she would fantasize her way through dysfunction. It was not until Piper was grown that she came to grips with the sneaky little things she had done.

> *The lust was already in me*
> *Forming like a disease*
> *Lying dormant for a while as if all is well*
> *Then the next thing I knew…welcome to hell.*

There was two boys Piper met on separate occasions. That seemed normal enough until it was on the steps inside the entrance to her apartment building. There were many entrances, on each end and in the middle of the long winding building. So, the staircase she met them at did not have a lot of traffic. They would talk but then it went to touching and kissing. It never went beyond that but for her age, which had to be maybe twelve/thirteen, it was dysfunctional. Piper was curious. But what Piper was unaware of was that she was yearning for the attention she no longer received from her dad. Both guys were a lot older than she.

> *My first encounter with love or so I thought*
> *Initiated an unfamiliar realm to be sought*
> *There had always been a void deep down inside*
> *Deficiency exploited what promiscuity supplied*

Piper and her sister eventually got the opportunity to live in another state with their dad. He got remarried to someone who had children of her own, her name was Ember. It gave her dad an opportunity to realize what he had been missing with his own children. The relationship formed between Piper and Ember led her to still feel abandoned because of the control her dad allowed Ember to have over him. Piper speculated that her dad allowed it, to make up for what he had done to her mother.

Piper, still yearning for male attention, met a guy named Louis who would become her first official boyfriend, but not before it got to a point where her dad decided to separate from Ember. The separation was meant to be temporary, but Piper savored every minute of being away from her stepmother.

After a couple of months, Piper's dad and stepmother began making up and they eventually reunited. Because Piper was involved in extracurricular activities, she begged her dad to let her stay where she was, which was in a different school district with his brother-in-law and family, and he did...at first. Looking back, Piper realized that her boyfriend Louis was a present help to get through the lack of relationship she was still experiencing with her, once again, absent dad.

After some time had passed and Piper felt comfortable, Ember convinced her dad that Piper needed to be under their rule, not her brothers. Not only did that make Pipers commute to school much longer, but it was also another reason to hold animosity towards her stepmother.

Piper's dad had gotten sick, Louis went out of state to college and though Piper had the accolades from school accomplishments, once again...she was not happy. Her unhappiness caused her to express her desire to return to live with her mom. To Pipers surprise, her dad asked her to give it more time before moving back and she obliged.

It was the summer of 84 when Piper decided she'd had enough. She hung around long enough to spend some quality time with Louis who was home for the summer. Leaving him was a difficult step to take because he was her first and not just boyfriend. He was the one she gave herself away to. He wanted her to stay but her frustrations outweighed everything else, so she decided to leave.

To be loved...we must be willing to receive love
To receive love...we must be willing to believe love.
To believe love...we must be willing to know love.
To know love...we must be willing

As Piper was gathering her things, Ember came into the room and asked Piper was she the reason Piper was leaving. As much as Piper wanted to scream "Hell Yes" …she could not. She just expressed how much she missed her mom and let it go. As eager as Piper was to get away from Ember, she was also heartbroken for having to leave the one person that was more than just a sister… Lola. Lola was her everything. Piper was on pins and needles until she returned home with her mom.

> *You warned me I must crawl before I walk*
> *Sometimes, I must listen before I talk*
> *So maybe fate isn't so mean…*
> *Before I can accomplish, I first must dream*

Piper was excited to see old friends and get back home. She started her senior year at the neighborhood high school but did not know anyone there. Around that same time, she had received news that her father Jasper had fallen down a flight of stairs and had been hospitalized. Upon speaking with him, Piper assumed his wounds would heal and he would return home.

That following weekend Piper and Ingrid attended a football game and that was where she got reacquainted with an old classmate from second grade, Deandre. The acquaintance turned into them being pretty much inseparable. After much persuading, Piper convinced Ingrid to transfer her to the same school her boyfriend Deandre attended.

After the Winter Formal Piper and Deandre attended, he stayed the night at Pipers house. The next morning while getting dressed, the doorbell rang. Pipers' mom answered the door. When Piper heard it was her cousin at the door, she thought it to be strange because he never visited before. His dad which was Pipers Uncle Kendrick lived in the same apartment complex. He advised her that his dad needed to see her right away.

Piper along with Deandre walked over to Uncle Kendricks apartment. When the door opened, Kendricks's girlfriend blurted out, "Ya daddy dead!" Piper gasped for air, covered her face, and began to cry. The family that had already arrived consoled her. Deandre did the best he could too. The shock was not so much in her dads dying. Their last conversation was him making peace with what he had done wrong with Piper and Ingrid. She knew what was coming. The shock she experienced came from the way she was told.

Ingrid did not publicly grieve, but she was heard crying in her room later that night. Turns out, there were a lot of questionable occurrences that surrounded Jasper's death and because Piper despised Ember, she did not attend the funeral. She was not alone in that decision. None of Jasper's family members attended either. A memorial service to honor his life was held where he and his siblings were raised, and all his family attended. As beautiful as it was, once again... Piper felt disappointed.

Pipers grieving process was rough because she would not allow herself to feel the pain of the loss. She asked her mom if Deandre could stay over one more night and Ingrid agreed. The next time Deandre slept away from Piper was when he went off to college.

Scenario 4

Forsaken

"The one, of many problems Lola faced was that she didn't have a clue as to what was best for her. How would she? It never got instilled by the ones who were responsible for doing so. For a long time, her choices flew under the radar of life or so she thought."

Lola was officially a preteen which was a big deal to her, especially as a new student. What she was unaware of was that it would be in this season that she would be forced to learn some vital life lessons that would alter the trajectory of her life.

By this time, Lola had made a great deal of friends at her new school and the area surrounding it, where she lived. There was one teenage boy, Austin, that would always ask her if she wanted some cat tail. Lola was only thirteen and had no clue what cat tail was, so she ignored him. Over several months, he would continue to cross her path and ask that same question, "do you want some cat tail", but Lola would laugh and shrug it off. The friends Lola made where she lived were from the "so called" hood. That was Lola's opinion of it because she had lived in much worse conditions.

One summer day, Lola's friend Cora, from down the hall called her and asked if she would come down to her apartment and hang out. Lola said yes and made her way over. When Lola arrived, Cora's boyfriend was in the living room with her. After the hello's, Cora asked Lola to get a cassette tape from her dresser in the room. Lola got up, walked into the room, and over to the dresser, and picked up the cassette.

As soon as she turned around, Austin was standing behind her. He shut the door. The door being shut must have alerted Cora in the living room to blast the music. It seemed like everything from that moment went in slow motion. Lola was grabbed and shoved on the bottom bunk of the bed. No matter how loud she screamed and hard she fought, that top bunk was keeping him and her contained. Austin took the one thing that Lola had control of. He took her innocence. Once he was done, he got up and went into the living room. Lola got up, ran out of the house, and went home. She did not tell anyone what happened that day. Three months later, Lola realized she was pregnant.

About your innocence
You should be able to reminisce
but impossible that is to do
When the ones you trust, violate you

When Lola turned fourteen, she was a freshman in high school and pregnant. She felt like she must have been the first one pregnant in school because no one there had a clue how to handle the situation. Neither did she.

Once Ingrid found out that Lola was pregnant, she suggested adoption, but Lola was not having it. She would rather leave her mom's house than put her child up for adoption, rape or otherwise. After giving birth at the age of fifteen, Lola got a job at a restaurant to support her child.

Since the occurrence, being fifteen with a child and living where they did, news traveled fast. The faster news traveled the more boys and men had it in their minds that Lola was easy. It also had a hold on how Lola handled herself and them as well.

Each thought provoking my mental state
Willing now, in this act…to participate
Assuring others that full is my cup
Ignoring the fact that my heart is becoming corrupt

"Little did Lola realize at that time in her life, the important role fathers were supposed to play in their daughter's lives to lead by example; the dos and don'ts of how a male should treat a female."

Jasper up to this point was nonexistent in Lola's life. He decided to leave and start a new life elsewhere however his siblings were still present in her life. Between Jasper's she experienced a larger family dynamic. Now with a son to care for, she welcomed the opportunity to get away from time to time.

Once Lola's son reached an age where he could go everywhere with her, around five or six months old, they would frequent relatives houses on weekends. One weekend, they hung out at a family gathering. There was this one close family friend that Lola thought was cool. His name was Clarence. He would let her drive his car, smoke a little weed, and even drink a little. But little did she know he had a hidden agenda.

Lola and her son Aiden had been hanging at the pool with family most of the morning. Taking advantage of everyone enjoying themselves outside, she decided to put him down for a nap. While they both were napping, Clarence crept into the room. As Lola was coming out of her slumber, she felt her bathing suit bottoms being tampered with then within seconds, penetration. By the time she realized what was happening, she was too scared to move. Her first thought was Aiden who was napping in the very same room. Not knowing how to respond, she laid there lifeless with tears saturating her pillow. Her frantic thoughts entertained the worst of what would happen if she told, to wondering who would believe her so just like the time before, she remained silent.

"Imagine being raped…twice before reaching adulthood, then, after all of that, still attempting to trust a man."

Why does this keep happening to me
God, why are you so mad at me
I thought monsters were a myth meant for fun
but to me, they came in the form of someone

Ingrid's choices in men did not exactly lead Lola in a positive direction. Ingrid had issues with men due to her father being nonexistent in her life. Ingrid dated but nothing that amounted to anything. Lola began noticing a distinct pattern between her mom's experiences and her own, so she made up in her mind that what happened was how it was supposed to be. Relationships came and went for Ingrid, all seeming to be based on sex, which Lola thought was the same thing as love.

"Lola befriended an older man who was the DJ of a teen club. Her mother allowed her to attend the teen club if he chaperoned her. It seemed normal at that time, given the previous dysfunction. The club had an age limit inside, with pedophiles outside."

At sixteen, Lola met a man, Huntly who was very persistent and careful. He moved slow, talked slow, and did not pressure Lola for anything. Lola became attracted to him, and they started dating. Seeing that Lola had already experienced the devil's nectar…it made sense that experimenting sexually would come easy for her. Between the rape, the molestation and the secrets kept, it seemed inevitable.

After a couple of months, Lola noticed the affect her escapades were having on Huntly. This grown man allowing her, a sixteen-year- old to put it on him. She had him too or was it that she was his first kid, and he could not resist. Either way, they did what they did for about a year. The only thing Lola took away from that experience was that he taught her how to please a man.

"Being a young girl and being molested has negative repercussions. It can affect a woman's perspective on what Love is and how a woman looks at a man and interprets a man's meaning of Love."

What exactly am I in search of?
I guess this would help, maybe it's love
All this woman that I have become
Why do I feel like I'm on the run?
Am I the only one craving constantly?
I hope it's not just me...

"You know that moment when the pressure of everything suppressed overtime comes to a tipping point? Well, what happened next altered the course of Lola's life once again."

Lola and Ingrid went to blows. Lola never held her tongue. Why would she? There seemed to be times when she had to be more mature than the decisions her mom was making. Lola was fed up with her mom's actions. Because Ingrid felt she could no longer chastise Lola, she reached out to Jasper and convinced him to let Lola and her son come and live with him and his family. Because Lola and Piper were so close, Piper decided to leave as well.

As if a part of me had become disconnected
My distorted thinking needed to be protected
Little did I know that the protection in need,
derived from the distorted part of me

The thought of moving somewhere new had Lola excited about her possibilities. She felt as if she was finally moving onward and upward. Lola, Aiden, and Piper took a flight to the west coast that arrived at night, so Lola's first glimpse was of the most incredible downtown skyline she had ever seen. The city was busy, even at night.

With Jasper being a cook by profession, there was nothing he could not cook. They arrived at Jasper's house, greeted with a smorgasbord of food and it did not disappoint. Cooking was the one and maybe even only thing Jasper prided himself on doing well. They had a two-bedroom apartment. Prior to arrival, Jasper and Ember already had three kids so adding three more people to share one room was a bit much to take in, nevertheless, she tried to make it work.

Intentions mean nothing
when reality is where we live...
So damn tired of giving and not living...
Expecting and not getting.

Dysfunction reared its ugly head once again as Lola's stepmom, Ember whom by the way, was in her twenties, attempted to take Lola and Piper out and show them the town. The evening began around the corner from the house. Ember and her female friend took Lola and Piper to an alternative lifestyle bar that had no age limit. Lola realized in that moment that she left one dysfunctional situation for another.

Lola was seventeen and no stranger to clubs by any means but was not feeling it at all. She expressed her disapproval, so they hopped on a bus and rode for what seemed like an eternity to another club. This club appeared to cater to teens, so she had a ball that night. Lola had also been introduced to Ember's sisters twenty- five-year-old male friend Bradford which seemed rather odd and pre-arranged. Between that and the bar thing, it left some concerns in Lola's mind, but she tried to make it work anyway.

Ember wanted Lola to apply for welfare for her and her son knowing that all the money would come to Ember. Lola disagreed, dropped out of high school, and got a job at a children's shoe store where Bradford was a manager. Jasper did not know immediately that she quit school and got a fulltime job. Once this was found out, Ember became upset because now she would not receive welfare money for Lola or her son.

> **"Lola being very outspoken, could no longer hold her peace about the things she had witnessed. In Lola's eyes, Ember wore the pants."**

Lola confronted Jasper about her perception of what was happening which made Ember angry, so they traded words. When Jasper would not defend himself, Lola got her son and walked out of the house to cool off. By the end of that day, Lola and Aiden had moved out of Jasper's house and moved in with Bradford. That ended up being her next traumatic experience.

Some time had passed, and it was still obvious that Ember had some sort of hold on Jasper. The one day he requested to see Lola, upon her arrival, she was approached at the door with a letter given to her by her dad that said he would not be responsible for any financial hardships she endured. It was signed and notarized. Lola had basically been handed her walking papers. Not only was she shocked, once again she was being abandoned by her father.

Time spent being wasted time
when things don't go our way
Is a ridiculous concept concerning life
dues we all must pay

From the time Lola moved in with Bradford, sex became a requirement at home, at work every day, at lunch, every night, and every morning. Then he ended up quitting his job. Lola continued working, still providing sex at home twice a day and taking care of her child.

One day, he and Lola got into an argument, and he cursed in front of Aiden, so Lola told him to watch what he said. That made him angry, so he grabbed her and put her and Aiden outside on the doorstep of the apartment. After sending her son to the neighbor's house, Lola went and got a spare key from the manager to get back in.

Once inside, Lola told him if he wants her and Aiden out then send them back to her mothers. When she said that, he grabbed her arm, put a belt around her wrist, and began pulling her so hard she hit her head on the frame of the door. When she came to, she was still being dragged by the belt around her wrist. Able to get free from the belt, as she got up, she noticed there was a clothes iron sitting on the counter. She grabbed it and hit him across the head, knocking him out. After all of that, she still stayed.

After everything calmed down, they talked it out and he promised not to try her again like that. Even though they worked that out they still struggled due to Lola being the only one working. With all the sex that took place, it was only a matter of time that Lola's second son would be conceived. Since her income could not take care of them all, they moved in with Bradford's mother, Ms. Tabitha.

> *What will it take to make true love come my way?*
> *I pray everyday*
> *Why does it seem like it's only me?*
> *I look around to see*
> *That special someone everyone has...but me*

Upon their arrival to Ms. Tabitha's house, there was already four sons living with her, so with Lola and her clan included, that totaled eight people under one roof. Though it was crowded, Lola enjoyed living there and took advantage of living rent free by attempting to get her diploma then college courses.

Lola took the exams and passed. Yay!!! She told Bradford and he got mad. She could not understand why. They got into an argument, so she and Aiden walked out to leave. The car Lola drove was a hoop-tie, so she had to add water to the radiator before she could drive it. When she went outside, he followed her, grabbed the water hose, put it over her head and drenched her in front of her son and his family. Lola and Aiden got in her car, wet and all. When she looked back in her rear-view mirror, she saw Bradford's van parked on the street by the end of the driveway. She put her car in reverse, turned to look at him, backed up going 25 miles an hour, smashed the hell out of his rear bumper then drove off. Bradford jumped in his car to follow her.

Lola drove headed to a nearby beach to clear her head and think things through. Suddenly, she saw Bradford's van pass by. He drove ahead of her enough to stop the van and get out. Lola looked at him, then looked at Aiden. She pressed the gas and burned rubber looking right at Bradford. She kept both hands on the steering wheel and headed right towards him to run his ass over. Lucky for him, he jumped out of the way. Lola looked in her rear view, gave him the middle finger and headed towards the beach and all of this was before she married him.

Wondering why situations are complicating my life
Trying to comprehend the meaning…while I'm feigning
for a way out and at the same time my mind is saying
I need to stop playing. This ain't no game…

During their stay with his family, their second son Marcellus was born. They decided to move into their own apartment. Once again, Lola ended up being the only working adult and managed to take care of the family. They lived there for approximately six months, then moved back in with Ms. Tabitha.

Lola and Bradford decided to make it legit and get married. It was a small wedding with just them, a witness, and the preacher. Ms. Tabitha was so excited to have Lola as a daughter in law. She and Lola became closer than peanut butter and jelly. Even though she could not hear or speak, Lola understood the sounds she would make to attempt to speak. Lola would help her with her bills, shopping, etc. so she did not mind them being there.

During Lola's bonding with her new mother-in-law, she and Jasper did not speak often, every now and then. His health began to deteriorate due to complications with diabetes. It did not help that he was a very stubborn man pertaining to his health. Since he was only in his forty's, Lola wondered if his current condition was his payback for abandoning her.

Half of Jasper's foot had to be amputated and from there it only got worse. He spent the last few months of his life in the hospital. Lola would go see him regularly to ensure he was not abandoned, like she was. Weeks went by with his memory beginning to fade.

One morning, Lola got a phone call from Ember informing her that Jasper had passed. Lola got in her car and hopped on the freeway trying to make her way there. It was raining and she had the radio on trying to keep her mind from wandering, but she finally lost it and cried the rest of the way there. When she walked into the hospital room, she saw him lying there with a white towel, rolled up and tucked under his chin to support his head. When she grabbed his hand, she looked at his palms, they were yellow and cold. She kissed his forehead and left the hospital.

While you were transitioning, I did all I could do.
But by then, you had reached the end of you
My emotions were like a clown with no makeup
for the first time I just wanted you to wake up

By that time, Lola was getting fed up with the life she was living and the direction it was not going in, so she decided to move back home with Ingrid. Her goal was to leave Bradford and take the kids with her, but he was not having it. He sold his car and all his belongings, then they took that long bus ride back to the east coast. It took three long days, but the closer they got the more excited Lola became at the thought of being back on "her" turf. When they arrived, they moved in with Ingrid to another full house because Piper and Deandre were also living there as well.

Scenario 5

Back to Life

"Lola was so happy to be back on her own turf. She had it all planned out to eventually divorce her husband shortly after she got home. He was now in the same position she was when she was on the west coast. No family, no friends only himself. Her goal was to get her shit together and move forward keeping in mind that on the west coast she had no one, but on the east coast she had it all."

In the mid 80's Lola got a job, bought a 76 Chevy Impala, blue with a white rag top and white interior. You could not tell her nothing. It felt so good. Bradford could not handle that version of her. When she was on his turf, she allowed herself to conform to survive but not anymore. Lola was back to her original self, and it felt marvelous."

This experience has me realizing what I don't want
I'm moving on, so you won't have to watch me flaunt
I refuse to continue to settle for less.
I gave my all…you should have given your best

A few months passed, and Lola and her family were still living with Ingrid. You would think that since they were on Lola's turf now, things would have gotten better concerning the treatment from Bradford, but it did not. One day Lola was going to a modeling search. She and Bradford agreed that she would take "HER" car to the appointment, and upon her return, he would be able to use "HER" car.

Well, they argued because he wanted to drop her off then pick her up. Lola disagreed. After getting dressed, Lola went to start her car, but it would not start. After several attempts to start it, Lola looked under the hood and her distributor cap had been snatched off, so she could not leave. Bradford was still up to his ignorant ways. If that was not bad enough, he hid the bag containing jewelry she was selling through a company she worked for. The arguments continued for days.

> **"Lola realized that some things are not controlled by man or woman. Destiny is only created and ordained by one, not some of us. Sometimes the answers you are looking for will not be revealed until you are ready to receive them. Just because you can't hear the answer doesn't mean God's not listening."**

Well, one day Ingrid made chicken and dumplings for dinner. No one had eaten yet. Bradford got hungry and went to make a plate, but since he did not eat dumplings, he proceeded to fill his plate with chicken only. Lola interrupted his attempt and told him how rude he was. His response demanded that she make him some damn chicken. That did not sit well with Lola. It did not help that Ingrid, Piper and Deandre were there at the time. So, she began making a joke about his command by saying "fry the chicken, fry the chicken, Buak Buak" (that is her chicken sound). Well before she knew it, he had thrown a raw piece of chicken at her.

Knowing she should have nipped it in the bud by calling the police on Bradford for a lot of previous reasons, his actions that day is what broke the camel's back. Lola proceeded to the pay phone in the complex and dialed 911. Before she could speak, Bradford hung the phone up. She began to walk back to the apartment and made it to the apartment door. There was a laundry facility right outside the apartment door. No sooner than she could reach for the door handle to open it, he snatched her in the laundry room and began choking her.

She tried to get him off but could not. Deandre must have heard her choking. He was an athlete, strong as an ox like you see on those body building commercials. Suddenly, Deandre walked in and said with his southern drawl, "Hey Partner, let her go". Since Deandre was so big, all Bradford could do was let her go. The police arrived, and Lola had them escort him out with his shit in trash bags. Lola did not care where he went or how he got there. All that mattered to her was his ass was GONE.

Sitting on the edge of my bed rocking back and forth
Contemplating divorce
Am I thinking too much into this thing?
Hell naw...it is time for a new beginning!

The answer is nope...Lola did not take him back. The only people he knew was Lola's family, so he moved in with Uncle Kendrick. They say birds of a feather flock together! No sooner after he moved in, he turned to drugs, probably to soothe his guilty conscience. Lola eventually moved from Ingrid's home to an apartment with her sister Piper.

It was the late 80's, and Lola was starting from scratch. No carpet, no blinds, no curtains. Boy, she was in for it. But at least she was on her own. Aiden's father Austin, the one that raped her, did not contribute at all in his son's upbringing, that was all on Lola. Bradford was not going to get off that easy, so Lola thought.

Lola and Bradford agreed that he would bring her money every Friday on his payday. Lola looked forward to it to take the strain off her to help with daycare, food etc. He made two payments without any issues. By the third payment, he began having excuses. He said his car engine went out and he would take care of this the following week. The following week came, then he lost his check. Lola's reasoning was that he should have borrowed or sold something until his check was replaced. She did not hear from him for years to come after that.

> **"Rape, sex slavery, drugs and alcohol among other things can confuse the mind and the body. Thinking or lack thereof about the how, when and the why when it comes to love affects the choice that needs to be made. When all that is available are negative experiences to draw from, it's no wonder that the outcome is detrimental."**

Lola did not live there much longer. She came home to a rat eating out of the spaghetti pot, so she decided to stop paying rent and stack her money to move out. Her stack did not have much time to grow because she came home one day, and all her belongings were on the curb. Lola felt like things were going from bad to worse. Thankfully, Deandre's mother, Ms. Vanessa lived right down the street. She allowed Lola and her kids to stay with her until things got better. Mind you, Vanessa already had multiple people living with her in a three-bedroom house. Nevertheless, Lola was so thankful.

Lola's life remained stagnant for a few months, but she refused to go backwards. Her only option was to keep it moving. She finally got a better job with a distinguished hotel downtown as a Reservations Agent and moved to an apartment in a nearby city with her sister Piper and a friend.

Around that same time, Lola, Piper, and their cousin, would frequent a restaurant turned nightclub at a well-known college. They had such good times; they met many good people from all walks of life. During their escapades there, Piper introduced Lola to who would become her third baby daddy. His name was Cooper. He was a college graduate that had a desire to get started in the entertainment business, he drove a BMW, had money, his own apartment. Lola thought she had hit the LOTTO.

When Lola and Cooper hooked up, it was a different kind of relationship for her. They were a couple, but not. Cooper wanted to control Lola but would not accept her as his woman. They would have sexual relations and that was it. It did not take long for Cooper to realize that Lola was not a yes girl.

Lola and Piper went to a male stripper show at a club. There was this one stripper, Jaylen who just so happened to be Cooper's frat brother. Lola knew him from that college campus club mentioned earlier. He came over to where they were sitting and did his stripper dance. Lola was under the influence and was determined to kiss him on his pretty butt cheek, so she did. They continued partying and had a great time.

Well, a couple of days later Lola got a visit from Cooper. Jaylen, the stripper called his Frat brother to tell him Lola kissed his ass... literally. He was highly upset. Lola had to put him in his place and remind him of the kind of relationship they had. No feelings, no commitment...so shut the hell up. He did not like that treatment, so he punched a hole in her wall.

I stood my ground because of the choices I made
Every choice I justified as a phase
Taking for granted all the while how I have been living
Never once considering the power I have been given

A few months later, Lola was pregnant with her third son Jaylen and yes...she named him after the stripper. Payback is a Be-Otch, isn't it? LOL Cooper ended up being no different than the others. He did not want to accept Jaylen as his son and take care of him unless Lola was giving him the cookie.

Lola and Cooper's relationship was a distant and mad one. Once Jaylen reached a few years old, Cooper started dating a friend of Pipers who knew Lola as well. The way Lola found out made her angry. To know that someone that close to the family would have no problem crossing that line left Lola furious. Cooper had no problem throwing it in Lola's face. That one act of betrayal ruined not only whatever it was that Lola and Cooper had going on but also the friendship between Piper and her friend. Some of Lola's blessings were blocked due to her not being willing to forgive them both, but this was not addressed until later in life.

> **"Lola realized that sometimes life can be a rollercoaster ride just like love. Situations come... some good and some bad. But no matter the situation, she chose to struggle towards the positive. Those positive thoughts and positive people brought about positive results. There were still some negatives, but it helped her snap back to life."**

It was the late 90's when Lola was introduced to her fourth sons' father, Sawyer by way of a card game played at Piper's house. Cooper on the other hand, had promised Jaylen a bike for his birthday, which was a few weeks prior. When he called and said he wanted to stop by, Lola thought he was bringing the bike. When he knocked, Lola answered the door and invited him and his friend in. Once Cooper saw who was in the apartment, it seemed like he was bothered and embarrassed at the same time. Lola asked where Jaylen's bike was. Cooper responded he did not have it. Lola snapped and kicked him out of the apartment. Jaylen finally got his bike a month after his birthday. The relationship between Cooper and Lola was very distant after that. She made it a point of making sure Jaylen had all he needed and some of what he wanted without the help from his father.

Years passed without any contact from Cooper. When Jaylen turned thirteen, his father wanted to play daddy, so he requested for Jaylen to come spend time with him for a couple of weeks over the summer. After a couple of days passed, Lola called Jaylen to see how things were going, since this was his first time away from her. Cooper grabbed the phone and told Lola not to call Jaylen while he was with him and hung up. Lola called back and Jaylen's grandmother answered the phone. Lola asked to speak with Jaylen, but she said he was not there. Lola was livid. She called Cooper back and said to him in a calm tone that increased in octaves as she proceeded, "If you don't have my son call me in five minutes, I'M TAKING A FLIGHT TO DETROIT AND I'M BLOWING UP YOU AND YOUR MOMMAS HOUSE". Lola did not play when it came to her babies. In her mind, Bih...For years you were not there and now you want to play daddy. Hell Naw!!

Now remember earlier, Lola and Piper were playing a card game with company, well it was with two male friends. One of them was Sawyer, baby daddy number four. Boy let me tell you. Lola thought it could not get any worse. She should have known better when he tried to buy tires with a clothing store credit card.

I realized that changes needed to be made
Because I made some choices, I thought I was saved
Without a renewing of the mind...all is pretense
Never once realizing I am still straddling the fence

Lola lived in the city with her kids and Ingrid. The apartments were nice when they first moved in, but two years after living there, they went downhill. Prostitutes, drug users and dealers soon took over.

Lola and Sawyer hooked up shortly after the incident with Cooper. He was much younger than she but seemed mature. They dated for a few months. Shortly after, in the late 90's, Lola was pregnant with her fourth son, Grayson. When Lola was six months pregnant, she went to her doctor's appointment and was advised that she had Chlamydia. Lola was devastated because she knew she was not the initiator. She cried for two hours then reminded herself that she was pregnant and had to remain calm. When Lola got home, she called Sawyer and told him the issue. The first thing that came out of his mouth was, "it wasn't me". Lola hung up. He called multiple times, but she did not answer. By day three he called, and she answered. Sawyer figured, it is better to tell the truth and maybe have a chance than to lie and not have a chance at all.

When Lola answered, all she had to say was hello. Basically, Sawyer said what had happened was, he was at a pool party and ran into an old flame from high school. The others decided to go to the store to grab drinks and food to grill. He and the flame stayed at the house to wait for other guests to arrive. One thing led to another and the next thing he knew, he penetrated her. Lola's thought immediately went to guessing that is what men mean when they claim they fell in some...you know the rest.

Then, to make Lola feel better, he claimed that as soon as he put it in, he thought about her and changed his mind. CHANGED YOUR DAMN MIND SHE SAID, hell, that was too late. At that point in Lola's pregnancy, she decided to leave it alone until she had her son. Even though they did not live together, Lola planned on moving before Grayson was born. Months after Grayson was born, Lola decided to end the relationship with Sawyer and be single, once again. She remained in sexual only relationships without the drama for years to come. When her needs were not being met, she decided to do something different.

> **"Lola's love attempted to make up for what she never received from the "supposed to be" most important man in her life...her father. As she dealt with men, all she had to go by was her past experiences. She began seeing the importance for a father to show his daughter how she should be treated. All she saw was how it shouldn't be."**

After going on a sabbatical for sixteen months due to her sexual wants and needs not being met, Lola decided to give a young man a chance. Yes, she was already a cougar, but "The Weed Man" was one of the youngest she had been with. His name was Dominic. She was fourteen years his senior and whether it be from sexual frustration or just missed the attention, Lola decided to jump in and give it a shot.

She met him through a friend that would usually grab her weed for her, but the friend was out of town and had advised Dominic that Lola would be stopping by. Lola really should have known better because he lived in an income-based complex. It should have dawned on her and maybe it did, and she just ignored it but, this apartment was not for single men selling drugs.

It was for woman and children who needed this type of housing. Lola walked in and Dominic looked at her like he was in a desert and Lola was a glass of water. He proceeded to serve her weed and at the same time asked her for her number. She spoke it real fast sort of hoping that he would not remember it and that would be her sign if he could not that it was not meant for her. Funny how you pay attention and believe in signs about bullshit but not signs from God.

Anyway, they went on a date and talked for a while, but she never asked him about his living situation because she already knew but did not want it confirmed. They continued relations for a couple of years.

There must be a daredevil inside of me
What about these dudes am I so intrigued to see?
From jump, I play by my own rules
So why in the hell am I the one still confused

Scenario 6

Wrong Choices

> "In 2005, the sisters, their kids and their mom moved in together. It was a large house that had 5 bedrooms that accommodated everyone. They all chipped in on the bills which allowed them to live comfortably."

Shortly after, Dominic moved in with Lola with the understanding that he would be responsible to help with the bills. Now, if you saw the movie named after a day of the week where the dealers friend asked him, "how you gon' sell weed and you smoke weed"? Well, obviously Dominic missed that part, because if he had, he maybe, just maybe, would have changed his thought process about it. Nevertheless, Lola put up with that type of mentality for months on end. Even though they shared a home together with 9 people, they got along ok.

The following year, the shit hit the fan over a $2.00 box of pizza. Lola truly regretted what happened that day because to her that situation separated her and Piper for years to come, in her mind. After grocery shopping, Piper's son Jeramiah ate a boxed pizza that Dominic bought. When Lola spoke to Piper about it, things escalated, and in the end, Piper moved out.

Lola later entertained the thought that if she were in her right mind, she would have put family before Dominic's sorry ass who did not pay bills yet got high all day, slept all day etc. But at the time, Lola chose to stand up for her so-called man. If she had to do it again, she would have told Dominic's sorry ass to eat a damn mayonnaise and ketchup sandwich. Lola and the rest of her clan did not stay much longer in the home because they could no longer handle the bills, so they moved to a condo. It was a four-bedroom condo, which Lola genuinely enjoyed except for Dominic's broken promises as far as helping with the bills.

Lola's tolerance had been nil to none when it came to men and bull-shit. But maybe it was her unresolved past trauma that kept her dealing with Dominic or maybe it was the free weed. At that time, Lola could not answer that for sure, but it was what it was. The relationship remained frustrating because of Dominic's lack of taking responsibility.

About a year later, Dominic took Lola's car after she told him he could not drive it. She did not realize it was gone until a friend stopped by and asked where her car was. Lola flipped as if she had lost her mind. She called Dominic up and demanded he bring her car back. That "Nicca" said NO! Lawd, snapping was about to happen. Lola hung the phone up, took all his belongings and threw them out the door, down three flights of stairs and called him and told him if her car wasn't parked in her lot in thirty minutes, she was reporting it stolen." Afraid of what he might walk in to, he knocked on the condo door twenty minutes later. Lola did not answer, he kept knocking and she kept not answering. He eventually left forty-five minutes later. Lola was happy and free once again.

> *I have had acquaintances I never really knew*
> *Sustained relationships that never really grew*
> *Not downplaying my past relations*
> *Just realizing that they were all infatuations*

Another year later, Ingrid, Lola and her kids moved to a house, which was cheaper than the condo. They had been there about three months when Lola met one of her co-workers, Miles on a personal level. He had a wonderful personality.

Lola was twelve years older than him, but no one could tell. They dated for a couple of months and began a sexual relationship. It was the evening of her birthday and Miles cancelled on her. Dominic called to wish Lola a Happy Birthday and yes, they hooked up. It was her birthday, and she was not letting it go without birthday sex.

Now, Miles came by the next day, and she had after birthday sex with him. Eight weeks later, she found out that she was pregnant at the age of forty-three. WTH!!! Distraught at the mere thought, she attended church with Piper whom by that time had begun mending the broken fence they had. Lola released her frustrations that day as she cried out, something Lola rarely did. She did not cry for long though because she knew better. In the meantime, Miles decided to move back up north so Lola did not see him again until about a year later. Dominic and Lola never got back together, that birthday sex was the last night they ever hooked up.

Now, in Lola's mind, Dominic was the father of her son Jameson, due to the timing in her mind. At the age of forty-three, Jameson was born healthy, and Dominic acknowledged himself as the father.

That year had passed and as Lola was sitting at her desk at the same company, guess who walks in for orientation, "MILES"! He stopped at her desk and saw a picture of Jameson. He asked Lola how old he was, at the time seven months. "He then asked if Jameson was his son. Lola told him no, but he demanded a blood test. Lola agreed because truly, she did not know either. Miles received the results and advised Lola that he was the baby daddy. Hallelujah!!!! Lola was relieved that she did not to have to deal with the Dominic anymore. Come to find out, Miles was even more excited.

"Lola reached a point in life where she realized that she was allowing herself to except certain treatments and levels of disrespect in her relationship. Sex does not mean Love and Love does not mean sex. Separating the two was difficult for Lola because she thought that if she was having sex, then she would fall in love only to find out that sex was overrated because she still could not get the fulfillment she was seeking. Realizing that made Lola change her thought process when it came to setting expectations about what she needed. Not what she wanted.

Scenario 7

What About Me

"After many failed attempts at what Piper thought love was, she ended up a single parent raising three kids by two different men. Her first son was born shortly after she turned eighteen. She was a teenager, pregnant in high school by the all-star athlete. All she knew is that she was pregnant and had no clue how to raise a child. She had made up in her mind that she would not hinder Deandre from pursuing his dream, so right before their first son was born, he left for college."

No faith…but faith was in need
Faith without works is dead indeed
No faith…no strength…just a pitiful excuse
to do whatever the flesh wanted to

Piper gave birth to her son with Lola, Ingrid, and Ms. Vanessa by her side. It was tough not having Deandre there. Piper had always pictured perfect moments, which in that case was him being present.

"Imagine that...as a first timer, Piper had no idea of what to expect with childbirth. She had seen the film on how babies are born, but it did not tell her about the fear and anxiety that came with it. Afterall, a human being was about to pass through her loins by way of her VAGINA! Though she had family members in the room, the biggest part of her still felt abandoned. Her fairy tale was not supposed to go like that."

Upon arriving home from the hospital, living in an all-adult condominium with her mom at that time, Piper asked Ingrid when they were going to move, as in Piper, her son Jr. and Ingrid. Her mom's response blew Piper away. Ingrid said she was not leaving; she did not have a baby. By that time, Piper had already resented some of her mom's choices subconsciously but that one hit her hard. It hit her hard because once again, she felt abandoned. Today Piper knows that was the best thing Ingrid could have done for her because it forced her to learn how to survive.

That was one of many letdowns that would occur. Shortly after the birth of her eight-pound five-ounce baby boy Jr., Piper was diagnosed with an STD that she had contracted while pregnant. Piper wondered how that could be possible. She had been faithful, and to make matters even worse, the STD had affected Jr. which was not immediately made known.

By that time, Piper, Lola, and a friend of theirs had moved in together. When Jr. was five months old, Piper began noticing that he could not hold down his formula. Not long after, he had broken out in legions all over his tiny little body. When Piper and Lola took him to the ER, the doctor gave a lame diagnosis and sent them on their way but not before drawing blood. By the time they got home, Ingrid was there informing them that the ER called and said Jr. had to be rushed to a different hospital.

When they arrived, the nursed immediately began a blood transfusion and a spinal tap. There were no words to accurately describe the excruciating scream that belted out of Jr. as they stuck that needle into his spine. To make matters worse, he was so chunky they could not find a vein, so they shaved a part of his head and placed an IV there.

You would have thought that Piper would have been livid about that happening, seeing that she had not strayed in her relationship with Deandre. Nope. Even then she was giving the benefit of the doubt that maybe he had contracted something through his athletic activities. Yeah, we know, go ahead, and say it. The doctor was very adamant in conveying that an STD is a SEXUALLY transmitted disease so unless he was having sex while performing athletic duties…well, you know the rest.

So, to break it all down, Deandre cheated on Piper while she was pregnant. He got diagnosed while she was pregnant. He got treated while she was pregnant. They stopped having sex before her third trimester, so he stayed cured. Piper carried her child and an STD the remainder of her pregnancy until she found out that day at the hospital. Her heart felt betrayed but not broken.

The question Piper was too uninformed to ask herself was, why not. Why wasn't her heart broken? Let us be clear, it felt broken in that moment but was treated as if it was nothing but a sprain. Broken things need mending. Piper did not mend anything. She just threw a band aid on it and kept it moving. It was easy to do since Deandre was away in college, still pursuing his dream. He never came home to deal with that issue. Piper had to have that conversation over a long-distance call at a payphone.

By the time Deandre came home for another visit, Piper and Deandre were a couple once again. She forgave him but looking back, the reason she went back was simply because she did not love herself enough to expect better. A year later, Piper and Jr. moved in with Ms. Vanessa. Piper's bond with her grew strong while living there.

Ms. Vanessa had five boys, so Piper became the daughter she did not have. Keeping it real, Ms. Vanessa became the mother Piper no longer had. Not because Ingrid had passed, but because Ingrid had decided to go out and live a little which did not leave much time for extended mothering.

> **"When Piper would think of weak, she immediately thought of defeat. That was the lie the enemy enticed her to believe and she took the bait. Because she took the bait without knowing God's promises for her...she became stagnant in what was supposed to be progress. But when she learned the truth, which is that God's strength is made perfect in her weakness, she was able to escape the pit her decisions put her in. Weak only equals defeat when chosen is to quit. Refusing to quit equips."**

About three years later, Piper and Deandre's second son, Jeramiah was conceived, Deandre and Piper were simply going through the motions in their relationship. Piper had stepped out on Deandre as well. The trust was gone on both sides. Lola and her then boyfriend let Piper stay with them until she birthed Jeramiah, then Piper officially moved into the low-income apartment she had been approved for. Brown Town is what they called it. Piper had grown up across the fence from it. This was the complex with the hole in the fence that the boys use to climb through. Piper saw it every day but never imagined she would end up living there. Not because she thought she was too good, just because she never thought it would be necessary.

The weekend Piper gave birth to Jeramiah, Lola and her boyfriend had gone out of town, so Piper stayed with Ingrid because she was close to her due date. Piper did not have insurance from work, and she did not qualify for Medicaid because she worked so she was forced to wait until her water broke before going to the ER, otherwise they would send her home.

> **"Imagine that...Piper sat in a car in the middle of the night for a couple of hours hoping her water would break so she could just lay down. Oh, the misery. But here she was once again, pregnant, and once again abandoned. Not by family but by the one whose presence she thought would have made all this a little more bearable. Seeing her daughter's frustration, Ingrid decided to pour water between Piper's legs to at least get her past the waiting area."**

Once admitted, it seemed like forever. The hospital only used natural methods to induce labor so twenty-two hours later, Piper finally gave birth to her beautiful nine-pound baby boy, Jeramiah.

Piper finally moved into her GOVERNMENT assisted apartment with her two sons, got on WELFARE and had the audacity to think she was finally independent. If that was not bad enough, she still tried to make it work with Deandre, but she eventually concluded that she was miserable...with him. So, she left.

> **"The worst of that problem was Piper's comfortableness with "IT". She was never physically or verbally abused yet the pain inflicted was obvious. The abuse she experienced was self- inflicted and worse, it flew under her own radar. If she had to give her form of abuse a name it would be called Lack. She lacked investing in herself, and she lacked a genuine love for herself."**

By that time Jeramiah turned eight months old, and Piper had reconnected with her first love, Louis. He invited her and the kids to visit him on the west coast. Piper accepted the invite. That was right before the Christmas of 88. It gave her a chance to put distance between Deandre and herself seeing that he was set to come home from college over the holidays. Plus, Piper needed to see Louis and make amends for the way she handled their breakup.

Piper and her boys stayed with him over the holidays. She and Louis were able to make amends while she and the boys enjoyed their holiday then returned home. It was no surprise that Deandre would be angry with Piper for leaving so they did not communicate with each other much. He was drafted in the sport he excelled in. Piper was happy for his accomplishment, given all that had been sacrificed so that he could pursue his dreams. Only problem with that was...Piper had forgotten about her own dreams.

What about me
What about what I want to be
A mother of two is my only identity
My plans were wrapped up in me and you
So now, what am I supposed to do

By the time Deandre got drafted, Piper was living in, yet another government assisted complex. Piper gives Deandre credit for asking her to find somewhere else to live, at his expense. But at that time, Piper did not feel comfortable moving somewhere that she knew "she" could not afford, should something happen to him.

When they were seniors in high school, Piper had a dream that Deandre had become an "avid drug user" and she never forgot that dream. She also experienced signs that confirmed suspicions while he was in college. So, while many may call it crazy for not taking advantage of the opportunity, Piper knew Deandre...and she was not wrong. After about two years, his professional career ended. What Piper did not recognize back then was the lack of faith she

49

had in herself to rise to the occasion using the opportunity Deandre extended to her.

So, Piper went on with life. She attempted to fill the void with lust filled encounters, and called it love. She went so far as to begin relations with the ex-boyfriend of a friend of hers, Shane. He was a summer fling but, in her mind, she had found The One. Piper became infatuated with him, mainly because he was everything Deandre was not. The only problem was that because her drug of choice to medicate herself was sex, that was all they were good at together. Since Piper was lousy with birth control, she ended up pregnant. She did not tell him that she was pregnant because to think that she would have another child and from a different man devastated her. She did not want to be a statistic. So, she made plans to have an abortion.

The date was set. Come that following Friday, in Piper's mind, all her troubles would be over, or so she thought. That Thursday Piper went to a job interview and on the way home, felt the sensation between her legs as if her water had broken. She soon realized that she was having a miscarriage.

Do not get it twisted, the relief she felt was absolutely nothing against her unborn child. It had everything to do with the ignorant way she handled herself and her business. Piper did not think she could afford to raise another child and then because it was with a man she had no vested relationship with, she did not want to deal with it…but God.

So, Piper confessed to Shane that she had been pregnant but miscarried. She also told Lola and Ingrid. Ingrid advised her to go get a D&C, but she did not. Shane made it a point to mention his disappointment over the miscarriage, but Piper was simply happy it was over.

Shane lived about an hour away, so he and Piper did not see much of each other once he returned to college. About a month later, Piper fell to her knees in pain, stomach pain to be exact. Lola rushed her to the emergency room. After some testing, Piper was advised that she was pregnant. Well, you already know she was in denial. Piper knew she had not had sex since the miscarriage. When she told the nurse that she'd had a miscarriage, they performed an ultrasound to show her there was a baby. The nurse explained that is was possible that she was carrying twins and lost one of the babies. Piper was shocked, to say the least but even worse, she now had to tell Shane that she was STILL pregnant.

Once Piper told him, the dynamics of their "relations" changed. She called it relations because they never made whatever they were to each other official. Piper heard rumors of his infidelity. She decided to confront him about it, seeing as she was carrying his child and they remained sexually active from time to time.

Piper took the liberty of confronting Shane while he was home for Thanksgiving. By then she was four months pregnant. Shane came home for the holiday and was visiting everyone but Piper. She demanded that he stop by so they could talk. He finally made it over but brought his brother with him. Trying to act as if nothing was wrong, Piper told him to take his brother home and come back. When he asked what they needed to talk about, Piper told him, "YOUR INFIDELITY" He tried to play it off and told her he would be back. The next time Piper saw Shane's face, their daughter was two years old.

When he said he would be back, he did not come back. He did not look back either. His mode of transportation was a moped, so when Piper would hear a cycle of any kind driving up, she would run to the window, hoping it was him, but it never was.

Lola was there, always there for Piper. She helped Piper with every-thing. She was there for the birth. So much so that as soon as Piper delivered, Lola grabbed Baby Girl and went off to a corner singing, "I love you, a bushel and a peck, a bushel and a peck, and a hug around the neck. I love you, yes, I do. I-love-you bum, bum, bum. The only girl out of the then five boys between Lola and Piper. So yes, she was spoiled.

Piper, on the other hand, was very bitter. But not bitter enough to find Shane or even go to his family and tell his business. Piper washed clothes at the laundry mat owned by Shane's grandmother. She even held Baby Girl, unaware that she was holding her great-granddaughter. Piper in that moment was so grateful that Lola did not know that Baby Girl was connected to the laundry mat owner. One can only imagine how that would have turned out. Piper just did what she had to do and made it work. But as for men, they were all dogs in her eyes.

"Life's journey preaches. Experience teaches. The value of life is based upon one's own perception. Piper went through a phase of believing that because she was a single parent with three children, that she was limited on what she could receive from a relationship with a man. She was on welfare and living in low-income housing. She figured men wanted what she offered, just not her."

By now it had been three years to the day that Shane's father abandoned them. It was Thanksgiving 1993. Lola and Piper had enjoyed the day's festivities, so it was time to party. Going clubbing was something they did regularly. The holiday made it something to look forward to, so they got extra fly. They were cute too!

It was not long after they got there and got a table that it got very crowded. There was a lot to look at. So, you can imagine Piper's surprise when she saw Shane stroll by. Piper's mouth dropped. As soon as she told Lola, Lola immediately got up and said she would be back. When she returned, she asked Piper to come with her. As they got outside and turned the corner, there Shane was. The moment had finally come for Piper to face her pain.

Scenario 8

What Happens Next

The Situation

"Not only had the sisters begun raising their beautiful children as single parents, but Ingrid also began living her life with the freedom she'd yearned for since divorcing Jasper. Ingrid's new lifestyle reinforced Lola and Piper's need to lean on each other."

It seems that both Lola and Piper had a lot of pain to face. They had to face themselves as well as what others had done to them over the years. As they moved further into relations with other men, the effects of abandonment became common, so they became comfortable choosing men that would eventually abandon them. They learned how to manipulate from being manipulated. They perfected being selfish amid their experiences with selfish people. They licked their painful wounds and even pulled back the scab during the process of trying to heal. They hid the shame, even from themselves. They allowed emotional instability to be their guiding force to the point of making choices without respecting the consequences that came with it.

Likened to a puzzle being put together one piece at a time, there are times when you can identify the missing piece and put it in place instantly. Then there are times when the piece you choose looks like it will fit but once you try it, you realize that it doesn't. Some pieces require little effort while others can take a long time to put together perfectly.

The puzzle represents life. The pieces represent situations. Putting them together correctly represent the solutions. The border represents the good and comfortable situations, easy to find and simple to put together. These situations represent one's adolescence. Most people love these pieces while others experience the unfortunate circumstances that leave scars instead of stars. Because these dark experiences remain unresolved, maturity stagnates and where confidence should have been, resentment resides and becomes the driving force for future decisions.

Over time, Lola and Piper came to the realization that there had to be better out there than what they were experiencing. So instead of searching for more excuses for their behavior, and the next man to fulfill some void in their lives, they, in their own time, began to do something different. Because they realized that through it all, they made it through, that something different.

The Solution

Believe it or not, solutions are available for every situation. Maybe not as we think they should but nonetheless, solutions are there. For example, in the book, Lola experienced rape. As if that was not bad enough, it happened during adolescence. She was not in control of the offense, but she was in control of the solution. One solution would be for her to allow her contempt for her accuser to remain buried deep within her. The contempt would then entice her future decisions to be made based upon what was inside her heart. The other solution would be for her to face her accuser, release her pain through trust in God's Word, pick herself up and use her experience to help others who have been offended.

When you seek God, what you receive is His guidance and a deeper insight of what life is and how it works. You don't get to see what is going to happen next, but you know that no matter how difficult the task becomes and how painful the outcome feels, because it serves God's plan...in the end, it was worth it. The beginning of wisdom is found in the formation of structure. Structure is necessary to propel to the next level of life.

So, it turns out that dream of them holding hands and never leaving each other behind was God's Plan. This is where Lola and Piper began their journey for a better version of life. With every experience they had from that point on, out of all the paths they took, only one led them to THE ANSWER. That answer came by way of the voicemail from their matriarch. After she heard raunchy lyrics on Piper's voice message talking about bumping and grinding, the words she spoke ended up saving their lives. She simply said, "Y'all Betta Consider God."

The Structure to Consider God

Lola and Piper began learning how to trust God with their hearts by allowing Him into those areas they were afraid to face. The subject matter that follows gives examples of what it took for the sisters to stop leaning on their own opinions about their circumstances and begin learning God's Word so that when they faced what was hiding in their hearts, they would be able to see it through His eyes.

Based upon what they learned, they began to align their choices with God's truth about them. Activating those truths in their hearts allowed them to begin following along the path God chose for them instead of the paths they chose for themselves.

> **"Allow your choice to Consider God to lead you on a journey to not only face but also dissect what has been hidden deep within your heart."**

Situations & Solutions

The Process

"The following topics represent what Lola and Piper had to face once they began dissecting what had become hidden deep within their hearts."

- **Relationship...**
  The state of being connected.
- **Abandonment...**
  Giving up on completely.
- **Manipulation...**
  Influencing cleverly or unfairly.
- **Pain...**
  Suffering and discomfort.
- **Shame...**
  Humiliation through consciousness of behavior.
- **Selfishness...**
  Concern with one's own personal profit.
- **Emotion...**
  A state of mind deriving from circumstances.
- **Disappointment...**
  Sadness from unfulfilled expectations.
- **Choice & Consequence...**
  The act of deciding and the result from that decision.

Relationship

The state of being connected

Lola and Piper struggled with establishing healthy relationships because the ones responsible for teaching and instilling those principles in them failed to do so. Lola's introduction to relationship started out on a sour note. She experienced rejection from out of the womb. The solid foundation she deserved was replaced with sinking sand.

The Situation

Most of what Lola experienced about relationship as a child was what not to do. Because her mother began displaying what would become a vicious cycle, Lola did the same. This paved the way for her to continue in years of dysfunction simply because she was never taught how to make a healthy connection.

As Lola got older, she would endure many battles within the relationship dynamic. With all the trust issues Lola adopted, a healthy relationship of her choosing was difficult to establish, the most important one being with God. All the trauma she witnessed and experienced literally convinced her that it was impossible to trust God. Not that He could not do it, she was convinced He would not do it for her.

The Solution

Relationships are hard enough when you can see the person you are in relationship with. Trying to establish one with the one you cannot see, but are still required to trust, takes faith. Faith is something God has given to everyone. If you do not believe me, think about all the negative situations believed in. Instead of Lola being prepared when her moment came to recognize God for herself, she could not.

Once Lola put forth the effort, she came to realize that genuine relationship with God was not much different than with a human. She first had to acknowledge God for who she heard He is, The Almighty God. Then she had to take time to get to know Him. She did that by reading His Word, the blueprint designed to answer every question she had. The answers were not obvious though. Her instructions to invite the Holy Spirit in deciphered the codes that kept her from finding the treasures inside of it.

Lola then began to set aside time just for God. Eventually their time together became intimate. It was within that intimacy that her comfort level allowed her to be vulnerable and transparent. She could feel herself beginning to trust God even more. That trust allowed her to see the importance of focusing on herself instead of being distracted by other people's mess. When she began focusing on her own mess, she began receiving God's Best.

When it all came together, Lola and Piper realized that all the struggles they endured had purpose, it provided the perfect opportunity to give God what He delights in...Their Praise. They found it difficult at first to praise God while they were going through things that felt tragic and hurtful. But as their time with God increased, so did revelation. They realized that struggle is opportunity for God to increase His existence in their lives. How much of Him they experienced depended upon how much faith they utilized.

We all get the same measure...the power is in how much of it we choose to use.

Abandonment

Giving up on completely

"It was drilled in Lola and Piper's head early on that the man was the head of the house and whatever he said is what it was. What they failed to differentiate was the type of man that privilege applied to."

The Situation

Abandonment caused Lola and Piper to question everything about themselves. It also caused a lot of other issues, likened to taking medicine then having side effects that cause you to have to take more medicine. Sitting back and watching the abandonment that took place was a major component that taught them to subconsciously accept it.

Abandonment took Lola and Piper on a journey that led them to their first stop…HOPE. The hope was that their individual situations would miraculously change, but it did not. That led them to the next stop…REJECTION. That was the "why don't you love me" phase. That long and winding road led them straight to ANGER. Anger justified everything they decided to say and do. Before long, they were sadistically entertaining memories of what they witnessed thus far, like the issues their mother Ingrid had with their dad Jasper whose lack of commitment to them both hardened not only Lola and Piper's minds but also their hearts. The sisters were left feeling vulnerable and insecure. It was in those feelings that they allowed their minds to entertain every thought the lack of love had whispered in their ear.

They were so focused on the disappointments caused that they never understood the importance to acknowledge within themselves the truth of the matter; they had abandoned themselves. The only thing left to do was something they had never done before…Consider God.

The Solution

Not yet knowing anything about a way of escape, when Piper's reaction to reading in the Word of God that there was one, stunned her. Up to that point, Lola and Piper's feelings of abandonment had taken a toll on their self-esteem to the point that they went searching for validation.

Eventually, the time came to do something different. Instead of continuing to beat themselves up about the pain, shame, and disappointment from feeling abandoned, through guidance they permitted themselves to learn who God said they are. Lola embraced the passage that said, "I AM FEARFULLY AND WONDERFULLY MADE." The scripture that really spoke to and fed Piper's spirit was the one where God said, "DO NOT FEAR, FOR I HAVE REDEEMED YOU."

It was amazing to Piper after she began reading the Word of God, why she clung to the power of lust over the love offered to her by her creator. But thanks be to God that Jesus Christ' dying on that cross and being resurrected covered every mistake they both made.

Gaining that understanding gave Lola and Piper free access to the adoption they learned was available in God's Word; all because they chose to believe it. That belief allowed them to override the lies of the enemy and believe every word God said about who they are and whose they are. The bottom line for Lola was in learning she was never abandoned because God had always been there for her. Her truth of the matter was that people disappoint...not God.

So how will you know when a person has your best interest at heart? Do not just listen to what they are saying to you. Anyone can fix their mouths to say anything. Start by learning the characteristics of Love. (I Corinthians:4-8) Knowing what love really is will help you identify when it is not. Signs are given, people just choose to pick the messages they want to listen to and apply to their lives. The ones ignored are usually the ones most important.

For those considering trying this, it does not happen overnight. Lola did not wake up to a completely different scenario. What she did do was seek God's truth, then she made the necessary mental adjustments which altered her route and before she knew it, not only was her thought pattern headed in a different direction, but she was also no longer yearning because she was not only chosen and accepted, she embraced that she was worthy of God's Best.

Manipulation

Influencing cleverly or unfairly

The Situation

Manipulation is one of those actions that becomes interpreted to serve as a means to an end. Since Ingrid never considered herself to be a selfish person, manipulation flew under the radar. Because it is not always consciously planned out, the ignorance of it convinced Ingrid to refer to it as a survival skill. Let us compare it to a toddler. They learn what works for them and what does not work for them and then behave accordingly. A baby learns early on that when they cry, they get the desired attention. Then they begin to manipulate what works. Well for Ingrid, that did not stop just because she learned how to express herself. In fact, it became easier for her to manipulate the introduction of what she wanted, rather than simply ask for what she wanted.

> **"Ingrid had no problem becoming outspoken to the point of saying whatever she wanted and believing that because she finally could that she was in control. What she had failed to realize was that she had no moral structure. She did not know The Word of God, so she was ignorant to all that was promised to her."**

The Solution

Because Ingrid was operating in manipulation, she was unable to move past a certain point in her life until she dealt with it. Ingrid had always avoided church and anything spiritual using the excuse that all church folk were hypocrites. That also gave her an excuse not to come face to face with the truth which required her to face herself.

For that moment to be effective, Ingrid had to love herself enough to accept the truth, then forgive herself for the part she played in the lie that she believed for years. It was extremely uncomfortable at first, because let's be honest, who likes being wrong? The excuses she gave herself to continue in that behavior did not stand a chance against the truth.

So, what is the truth you might ask? The truth is that there is an enemy that would love nothing more than to devour you. Scripture says that deceivers shall eat of the fruit of their own way and be filled with their own devices. Ingrid's behavior gave the enemy every opportunity to steal her purpose, kill her dreams, and destroy her future. He was so smooth that he did it in a way he knew would make her comfortable receiving, not her demise, just the pathway to it. Thanks be to God for providing a way of escape. That way is not Ingrid's truth, not your truth, Jesus (the Living Word of God) is The Truth.

> **"God's Grace was not permission for Ingrid or anyone else to do whatever is wanted. It is the way of escape from the enemy's grip. See... once Ingrid realized that all she was responsible for DOING was making the right choice, the check was covered."**

Pain

Suffering or discomfort

"The pain Lola and Piper experienced was psychological. For them both, it was one of the most damaging feelings ever experienced. While unchecked, it caused every decision they made to be based out of pain. Like the hidden buried emotions, they could not deal with because they were not taught how to."

The Situation

Lola and Piper equated pain with a feeling. While physical pain is felt, emotional pain, on the other hand, begins with a single thought. Piper chose to entertain those thoughts that were painful.

Every attempt Lola made to feel better felt like her body was stuffed with cotton. She tried to feel better but could not. She walked with shame at first thinking everyone could see the pain. She felt like she had an odor and people could smell her. When boys and men would look at her, her first thought was they were going to take something from her. Pain was instant for her; not something that started slowly then grew massive. So, when her decisions were made, they were instant the same way her experiences gave it to her."

Pain is uncomfortable and it hurts. That alone would cause anyone's instinct to advise them to…RUN! Pain is universally known as an enemy. Pain signifies that something bad is happening or has already happened. The unchecked "already happened" kind of pain usually leaves one feeling like they are stuck without knowing why. Leaving it unchecked entices medicating instead of meditating. Take a pain pill for instance. Pain pills do not heal, they only numb.

The problem is that when that numbness wears off (and it always does) the pain is once again, staring you in the face. The pain that signifies "something is happening" is the warning sign to get help. Deciding not to get help uncovers the paths that can be taken. This is where that enemy spoken of previously will entice you to entertain every reason you cannot get your healing. That path usually ends in a ditch which feels impossible to get out of alone.

> **"Lola tried licking the wounds God was waiting on permission to heal. Because she did not know God would heal them, what she was choosing was keeping her in a destructive pattern that kept those wounds open. In other words, she was sitting in a mental prison cell with the door wide open."**

The Solution

As crazy as it may sound, the solution to overcoming pain is in facing it. The reason the solution is hidden in the pain instead of being obvious is because as God's Word says, "His strength is made perfect in our weakness." That means you must seek Him. Choosing not to seek Him makes His strength appear nonexistent because of the lack of faith. A believer knows that Gods strength is sometimes camouflaged within the pain nonetheless, the only way out is by finding the door (which is God) and walking through it. Otherwise, you stay there, unable to go any further.

Lola and Piper had a choice to make. They chose to refuse to entertain the enemy's shenanigans, so they changed who they allowed to control the narrative in their minds. Instead of entertaining the enemy's lies, they chose to believe God's Word and trust His plan.

Facing pain does expose weakness. But that weakness is necessary to witness God's Strength working on your behalf. Once you experience it and acknowledge that it is God's doing, you learn and become comfortable with how to go to God and give Him every burden. Just remember, depending on God does not cause the problems of life to cease. What it does is allow you to take rest and be at peace during them because it is God's Plan you can now begin to trust.

> **"When Lola heard the word "broken", the first thought that would come to mind was pain. What she had not yet realized was that brokenness before God meant that she had finally surrendered trying to heal her wounds her way. Lola found God at the end of herself, henceforth the best position to be in."**

Shame

Humiliation caused by the consciousness of behavior

"Piper struggled for a long time because she had not yet been formally introduced to the understanding of grace. She beat herself up and had nearly convinced herself that she would never receive the best of anything because of her past mistakes. It was difficult to discipline herself because for a long time, what she thought she wanted she could have with no regard to the consequences that came with her decisions. Not big things, the little things that were kept a secret and flew under the radar. The ones nobody would ever guess. Then it hit her…God knows."

The Situation

For a good portion of her adult life, Piper struggled with shame. Not so much outwardly. She knew how to wear the mask. Hell, she dressed the mask up to perfection. The mask displayed a woman who brought home the bacon and fried it up, cleaned the house,

70

provided for the kids, and knew how to be cute when it was time to. But inwardly, Piper was beating herself up. She felt inferior about the sneaky things done behind closed doors. Things that only she and who she did it with knew about, or so she thought.

Shame kept Piper thinking she was not worthy of the best of anything. Shame convinced her that a single parent of three children living in low-income housing and on welfare would never find true happiness. So, Piper settled for what was comfortable based upon past experiences. She stayed there for a long time. That was one of the stayed stuck moments, until she faced it.

"Until Piper realized whose she was, she could not value who she was. Because she had no insight into that knowledge, she gave herself away, and when she did, it was not even to the highest bidder. She just wanted to feel better, even if it was temporary. She was desperate for affection and the only kind she knew about was of the physical nature. When she felt emptiness, she would go searching for someone to fill it, completely unaware at that time that some places are reserved only for God."

The Solution

Piper learned that to overcome shame, she had to change her pattern of thinking. The first valuable lesson Piper learned was that she was not what she had done. She made mistakes, but she was not a mistake. She treated herself as if she was the mistake. She judged herself unaware that God covered her mistakes when Jesus got up on that cross and died. He died for every sin, not just some of them.

When Piper realized her sins were included, the gratitude towards God for doing so led her to begin learning how to be more confident within. That confidence granted her access to put just as much, if not more faith in God's truth as she had done with the enemy's lies. That processed began exposing the enemy's hiding places within her which is how he would remind her of her past mistakes. Piper learned to change the channel…in her mind.

> **"After so much disappointment, Piper had convinced herself that what the enemy dangled before her was truth. The lightbulb that finally came on was not in her head but in her heart. She had to learn how to be fully persuaded and allow herself the opportunity to thrive on God's promises because they included her."**

Selfishness

Concerned chiefly with one's own personal profit

"The sisters being selfish through their actions became nothing new to them. It wasn't new because it was a learned behavior. Every negative experience was introduced by selfish people. It was a part of life, and they became numb to it."

The Situation

The deception connected to selfishness is that it can fly under the radar. That radar spoken of includes those closest to Lola and Piper whom they were under the impression could be trusted to lead by example. Turns out, what Lola and Piper experienced was that those closest to them influenced their thoughts so that their own personal profit could be gained.

The worst part of selfishness is that it goes undetected by the person being taken advantage of. That is what happens when true intention is masked. It gets dolled up to be pleasing to the I. (not eye but I), because that is the only person selfishness is loyal to.

It began with being taken advantage of. Once the seed of selfishness was planted, the weeds began to grow. Open windows led to open doors. That learned behavior taught Lola and Piper to become a product of their own environment. Being selfish did not stop with what they did to others, even worse, what they did to themselves.

> **"Where there is no portrayal of unselfishness, the chance of becoming the opposite is easier. Selfishness is a learned behavior much like manipulation. As stated previously, they go hand in hand. The sisters learned how to be selfish from the experiences in their lives. Them not realizing what selfishness was, made them feel ignorant to its devices when they got older."**

The Solution

There is a scripture that says, "Search me oh God, and know my heart." When that is asked, one's own selfishness comes to the surface, and it initiates the process of everything else associated with it that needs to be surrendered. Once at the surface, the opportunity is afforded to recognize selfishness for what it is, then surrender the behavior to God with the mindset of changing.

Are you wondering how it will be recognized when it comes to the surface? Well, for Lola and Piper it came on separate occasions from people who loved them enough to give them the truth. Of course, they both were in denial at first, but through examples given they were able to see the deception they caused themselves. That truth offered Lola and Piper the desire to do right instead of desiring to be right (in their own eyes) as they took the necessary steps to become a better version of themselves.

Emotion

A state of mind deriving from one's circumstances

"Lola's experiences of betrayal came from her being violated. Being violated produced moral and psychological conflict within herself and her relationships. Talk about a roller coaster ride. She felt like she was going 100 MPH on a constant down slope. The whole time...she was mad as hell."

The Situation

For Lola, she was able to stick all her vulnerable emotions in a box, lock the box then hide the key. For Piper, it was impossible to control her emotions without a foundation to stand on. But oh, how she tried. It would appear to be controlled for a while, but as soon as Piper got comfortable, that ship started sinking. While uncontrolled, Piper made it easy for emotions to control her instead of her regulating them. When she felt hurt, it became agonizing. When she felt fear, it became paralyzing. When she felt angry, it became irritating. When she felt sad, it became discouraging. When she felt happy, it was only temporary.

What Piper had not yet learned was that those emotions were like a toxic acquaintance. At first it seemed a necessary part of the process but overtime it drained her. The reason the negative emotions lingered for as long as they did was because she never used her authority, "she" had to change her mindset.

Pipers' emotions and Lola's lack of emotions affected how they thought, felt, and acted. It also helped determine how they handled stress, how they related to others, and made the choices they made. At every stage of their lives, from childhood to adolescence through adulthood, there were so many emotions Piper experienced yet Lola chose not to indulge.

Just when they thought things would get better, it never failed. Once again, they would be faced with disappointment which for both still turned into denial which turned into regret.

> **"Not realizing it then but God was in the midst because there was a tiny bit of hope that Lola and Piper held on to. Hope was all they had to keep themselves going. Hope that there was a bright horizon and grass that would be greener on the other side."**

The Solution

Emotions serve a purpose. They provide information likened to our senses. They are usually triggered by circumstance. What Lola and Piper learned through process of elimination was that it is a human experience to get angry, be hurt, be disappointed, be sad and even scared. What emotions are not supposed to do is linger. Kind of like a broken leg, who leaves a broken leg broke? Who allows a broken leg to go untreated?

The first thing to do is get treated, and not just by anybody. You do not go to a mechanic to fix a broken leg. You go to a specialist. Someone who knows exactly what to do. You get it done so that you do not become handicapped in that area. It was time for them to treat their emotions the same way.

Piper had to stop beating herself up because she was emotional. Lola had to trust God enough to release the emotions she had locked away. Once they began doing that, with the help of someone who specialized in that area, Lola and Piper learned how to put them and keep them in perspective.

"There is a feeling greater than any other feeling. Knowing that the relationship the sisters were beginning to have with God could not be matched, there was no competition with anyone else. Even better than that, they realized that He always had and still has their back. No more abandonment, no more manipulation, no more selfishness, no more pain, no more shame, no more emotional roller coasters, not because they no longer exist. All because they have decided to Consider God."

Disappointment

Sadness caused by the nonfulfillment of expectations

"The beginning of Piper's existence was filled with daddy daughter moments that strengthened her belief in being protected and provided for. When it was stripped away, Piper's assurance in her identity left a gaping hole in her mind and in her heart."

The Situation

Piper struggled to understand why her dad was willing to disconnect their bond. Did he not know how his decision would affect her? Piper went from being confident to fearful because who she relied on left her. She had become wounded with no idea how to care for it, so she did nothing and like an untreated wound, it got infected. Over the years, that infection affected her thoughts, her emotions, as well as her decisions. Then as she grew to know who God is, she became disappointed when she found out that God allowed it. She became unsure and insecure.

The Solution

Through process, Piper realized that her foundation was never supposed to be her dad, he was supposed to introduce her to her foundation which is Jesus Christ, The Living Word of God. Jasper was granted the opportunity to teach Piper who her foundation is before he died. Knowing that helped Piper realize that for every hurtful woe she had to endure, there was a valuable lesson to be learned from it. It was in that lesson that she was made wiser, stronger, and better. Piper understood it even more when she realized that she was no longer living for herself, but for Christ.

Disappointments are a part of life. How they are dealt with is an indicator of where we are in our walk with God as opposed to where we want others to think we are. Piper chose to remember that with God, there is always a purpose for whatever He allows. It is up to us to choose to trust Gods Plan.

Choice & Consequence

*The act of deciding and the
result from that decision*

The Situation

**"What Lola struggled to understand was why
the people who made horrible choices con-
cerning her, made them. WHO GAVE THEM
THE RIGHT, that right which was taken from
her?"**

Lola became less concerned about her choices when it came to nega-
tive behavior. She thought she was taking her right back based upon
those choices. Lola rationalized that by saying yes, it meant they were
no longer taking from her, she was giving and because she was "giv-
ing" herself away, that meant she was in control and that made her
feel better about the act itself.

Lola's choices were swayed by her unresolved issues and unmet needs.
Choices that were made because of her negative experiences failed to
allow her to overcome them. Instead, she was influenced by them.
Lola needed a foundation that would assist her with her choices. That
foundation came with learning the ultimate sacrifice Jesus made with
His choice. He did not deserve to be brutally beaten, degraded, and

He certainly did not deserve to die, but He did because despite all the pain, He endured it remaining focused on The Purpose.

Lola had to make a choice to find a way to shift from reaping negative consequences to sowing good seed so that she would eventually reap the good. God's Words says that a man reaps what he sows', so to eventually reap the positive, she had to plant her feet and stand firm on what she was learning to be true, to exhibit to others the same unconditional love that God was extending to her.

The Solution

"Lola was beginning to observe her power to choose based upon the experiences she had. She began respecting her ability to make a choice knowing that for every choice, there would be an action, for every action, a reaction and for every reaction, a consequence."

Choice is one of the most important responsibilities we have. Believe it or not, there is a choice to be made in every circumstance. That means, whether the choice is initiated by you or the response of something that has happened to you, there is still a choice that must be made. That choice determines what direction you will go in.

You may be asking how to make the right choice when the proper tools have not been instilled. Well, when you have a question you earnestly desire to know the answer to, you seek to find that answer. This is the importance of studying and applying God's Word to our lives. Once we nourish ourselves with God's Word, we make wiser choices because of the abundance of wisdom we embrace.

When Lola was not acknowledging God, he was still there. His word says that even when you make your bed in hell, He is there, still providing a hedge of protection. Maybe not the kind Lola preferred but as she kept on surviving, she chose to see that He had been in the midst the whole time.

Because thoughts have been granted Free Will by God himself, it means that there is a choice to make. The wisest choice starts by bringing every thought captive to the obedience of Christ Jesus... The Living Word of God.

Consider God…

Trust in the Lord with all thine heart.
And lean not unto thine own understanding.
In all thy ways acknowledge him, and he shall
direct thy paths. (Proverbs 3:5-6) KJV

"The remaining topics represent what Lola and Piper allowed themselves to receive and walk in upon engraving the truth of God's Word in their hearts."

- **Confession…**
  An admittance of guilt.
- **Forgiveness…**
  The cancellation of any form of debt.
- **Faith…**
  The substance of hope, evidence of what is yet seen.
- **Hope…**
  An optimistic mindset expecting positive outcome.
- **Love…**
  The Word of God in action.

Confession

An admittance of guilt

**If we confess our sins, he is faithful and just
and will forgive us our sins and purify us from
all unrighteousness. 1 John 1:9 NIV**

Confession for Lola and Piper was trusting God with not only their offenses but also their mistakes. Once they acknowledged their wrongdoing, they did not stop there. Confession continued by Lola and Piper cleaning out their own separate internal closets because containing all the hurt, pain and shame offered no capacity for cleansing.

**Therefore, if anyone cleanses himself from what is
dishonorable, he will be a vessel for honorable use,
set apart as holy, useful to the master of the house,
ready for every good work. 2 Timothy 2:21 ESV**

Transformation

Once Lola and Piper finally observed their former behavior for what it was, they were able to truthfully identify the sin and agree with God about it instead of continuing to justify their behavior. Their choice to do that freed them from the dread and concern of their past. To get beyond that place, they had to Consider God.

Confession was not them telling God something He did not already know. God sees EVERYTHING! Confession was and still is for their/our benefit. It allowed them to expose what had become a hiding place for the enemy who lingered in their secrets and hid himself from them...in them.

Whoever conceals his transgressions will not prosper, but he who confesses and forsakes them will obtain mercy. Proverbs 28:13 ESV

That is why it became important to learn how to be transparent. Every secret Lola and Piper exposed became an eviction notice to the enemy. He could no longer hold them hostage in their hearts nor in their minds. It did not mean they told everyone their business. They confessed their wrongdoing, asked God for forgiveness then changed their mindset.

Up Against the Wall

It is time I put down my pride, get down on my knees and pray to YOU. I ask YOU Lord to forgive me for all the wrong that I do. The thought of exposing my dirt gives me doubt, it is such an uncomfortable thing to talk about, but I am up against a wall. Everyone who knows you says all I need to do is call.

So, I call on Your Name needing to know if I confess today, what happens tomorrow? Will I really be able to see all those things that once blinded me? Will I stand unashamed and give my testimony on how YOU made a way out of no way for me? When obstacles come, will I still drink from your cup? In passing conversation, will I bring YOU up? Will I, through faith, no longer have doubt? Through my lifestyle, tell what YOU are all about.

As I learn each day the right things to do, since YOU said yourself that I can come to you and You would give me rest; then I say yes, and I confess that from this day forth, on your name I will call and not just when I am up against a wall.

Forgiveness

The cancellation of any form of debt

And whenever you stand praying,
Forgive if you have anything against anyone,
so that your father also who is in heaven
may forgive you your trespasses.
Mark 11:25 ESV

Piper went into her room with her door closed. She set the scene with dim lighting, with praise and worship softly playing. She began talking to God, like I am talking to you now. She began telling Him about her day, not because she did not think He already knew but because she needed to release the concerns she had.

After Piper finished talking, she began singing to the music. That led her to get caught up in her praise to God. She began to cry, but not tears of agony nor defeat. The tears were a product of her praise. Her praise came from reminiscing about situations God delivered her out of. It was a beautiful experience.

Then it happened. It came out of what seemed to be nowhere. While caught up, a person came to Piper's mind. She would be lying if she said she remembered who it was. You will understand why in a minute. So, when that person came to her mind, the next words out of her mouth was, "Father, I forgive them". Then another person came to her mind, so she told God that she forgave them too. Then another came to mind, and another. By the time it was over, Piper had cancelled the debts of all the people she thought owed her something. She made up in her mind that she was going to release them which in turn really released her from the bondage that kept her caged mentally.

Once Piper was done, the moment then shifted to her asking God for forgiveness for all the things that she had done to others. Still caught up in the moment, she then began to forgive herself for staying comfortable in the mental cage for so long. Piper had heard it before that forgiveness is not for the other person, it was for her. IT FREED HER! It cleansed her. Even if the other person did not accept it, Piper had done her part. Why you ask? Because God cancelled her debt when Jesus died. The very least she could do was the same.

At The Cross

At the cross, is where I lost my sinful nature. A renewed creature, possibly even a teacher...God Willing! At the cross, no longer tossed to and fro because now I know who to follow when time to go, who to exude when time to show, who to listen to when time to hear and who to call on in time of fear.

At the cross, Jesus paid the ultimate cost for every human being's sin. Oh, if only we would follow Him. He is the only door to salvation. He who was before creation, came to earth and redeemed the lost.

Completely glorified...At the Cross

Faith

The substance of hope, evidence of what is yet seen

Lola and Piper always thought they had faith because they said they did. What they did not know was that though faith is given to everyone, it requires relationship with God to sustain it properly.

> *"For by grace you have been saved through faith.*
> *And this is not your own doing; it is the gift of God,*
> *not a result of works, so that no one may boast."*
> *Ephesians 2:8-9 ESV*

So, when that lightbulb finally came on, they realized that, in the same way they would not allow themselves to trust a stranger, they would not allow themselves to trust God because they never took the time to get to know Him. Lola and Piper learned that with every experience they encountered, they were being prepared to utilize the faith given to them by God.

"And without faith it is impossible to please him, for whoever would draw near to God must believe that he exists and that he rewards those who seek him. Hebrews 11:6 ESV

There were many uncomfortable moments while they were walking through it, but once it was over, they were always better for the experience. It gave them the opportunity to watch God, not do it their way or in their time frame. Most times, God did not give them what they thought they wanted. Hallelujah!!!!

What Lola and Piper encountered was God's Word being fulfilled in their circumstances. So, when they felt pain, faith showed them that it had purpose. When they felt rejection, faith showed them that whoever was rejecting them was not meant to continue the journey with them. When they felt violated, faith showed them the power of recovery and how it would someday give someone else the strength to overcome. They basically saw for themselves what God's Word says, "FAITH IS THE SUBSTANCE OF THINGS HOPED FOR AND THE EVIDENCE OF THINGS NOT YET SEEN."

"So, faith comes from hearing,
and hearing through the word of Christ."
Romans 10:17 ESV

Hope

An optimistic mindset expecting positive outcome

It is easy to give up when hope has vanished. The first thing to do to solve that problem is finding out where hope comes from. Our hope comes from God.

"May the God of hope fill you with all joy and peace in believing, so that by the power of the Holy Spirit you may abound in hope."
Romans 15:13 ESV

Lola and Piper's hope was not being utilized because they assumed to know what was best for them. When what they thought would happen did not, they went out of their way to try to make it happen anyway. Some of those ways required of them to lay aside their morals and values which in turn sent them down the rabbit's hole of disfunction. Lola and Pipers hope stalled from desiring what they eventually became comfortable with.

Hope is not meant to be measured by what we go through. Hope is eternal because the one providing it is eternal. That means that no matter what we go through, hope is always present; it is a choice we must make whether to hold on to hope or lay down and die.

What they were completely unaware of at that time, was the blueprint that had always been available to them. That blueprint was and still is The Word of God, filled with a plethora of hope for anyone willing to believe. Hope is the optimistic view one can choose to take because they stand on the Word of God and His Promises. His word says that He provides a way of escape and that He will not put more on us than we can bear. There is a handful of hope right there. The problem Lola and Piper faced was in not knowing what promises were available to them.

There is a saying, "You can't win if you don't play." Well, you cannot stand firm where there is no foundation laid. Lola and Piper grabbed hope by the hand and eventually took God at His word when He said...

"TRY ME AND SEE."

"For you, O Lord, are my hope, my trust, O Lord, from my youth." Psalm 71:5 ESV

Love

The word of God in action

***And now these three remain: Faith, Hope, and
Love, but the greatest of these is LOVE.***
1 Corinthians 13:13 NIV

What is Love? Many including myself use to think that Love was a feeling to later find out that is called infatuation. Love is the action displayed that produces positive results. Love started out difficult for Lola and Piper. They could say it was because they were around some people who displayed what love was not, but then they would be lying. However, they did believe that love included the negative they witnessed. That mindset allowed them to be comfortable in the behavior attached to it. So comfortable, that they failed to see what was wrong with it in the first place. Their misunderstanding about love was not just directed towards others, they did not know how to love themselves either. That was the biggest betrayal of all.

Lola and Piper eventually learning that God is Love clarified why they were not willing to fight for what was right concerning their lives. Not yet knowing God on a personal level permitted them to be comfortable dwelling in and amongst the lie rather than take a chance on understanding the truth…But God!

True love requires transparency because The Word of God is just that, transparent. It simply means that when face to face with every option, choose what is right in God's Eyes, not your eyes. Lola and Piper chose the truth in God's Eyes over the lie. Why? Because God is love, love is an action, not what we say, love is what we do.

"Love is patient and kind.
Love does not envy or boast,
it is not arrogant or rude.
It does not insist on its own way.
It is not irritable or resentful.
It does not rejoice at wrongdoing
but rejoices with the truth."
1 Corinthians 13:4-6 ESV

Last, but Not Least...

Trust in the LORD forever,
for the LORD, the LORD himself,
is the Rock eternal.
Isaiah 26:4 NIV

So grateful are Lola and Piper now, to know what direction to go in. What the enemy dangled before them, could have taken them out completely. But instead, they eventually ran to God's hiding place. They found His hiding place by accepting the Grace and Mercy extended to them, but not just for them, for the ones they adore also. That was and still is the beauty of it all.

While Lola and Piper do not know the future, trusting God's plan is what has been proven to give them peace. Even when the result was different from what they prayed, they decided to trust that the decisions they make in the future, are ones that line up with God's Will for their lives.

The Declaration…

With God on my side…I don't ask why.
With God on my side…I refuse to hide.
With God on my side…I fear no man.
With God on my side…
I do all that I can to reach out and help my fellow man.
With God on my side…there is no option to fail.
His blessing from day to day is how I prevail.
Since on my side is HE, forever grateful I will be.
Not just for watching over me.
Being my eyes when I chose not to see.
But also, for being someone in whom I confide.
For teaching me lessons with the tears I have cried.
Cause the reason I am still alive
Is because God is always…ON MY SIDE!!!

www.ingramcontent.com/pod-product-compliance
Lightning Source LLC
Chambersburg PA
CBHW071024120626
46546CB00003B/1212